A
Northamptonshire
Lad

Arthur Sturgess' parents, William and Elizabeth, about 1929.

A Northamptonshire Lad

ARTHUR STURGESS

Northamptonshire Libraries
1982

Published by
NORTHAMPTONSHIRE LIBRARIES
27, Guildhall Road, Northampton NN1 1EF

ISBN   0 905391 09 8

Designed by Bernard Crossland Associates.
Printed in Great Britain at The Alden Press
Oxford, London and Northampton

CONTENTS

ACKNOWLEDGEMENTS

Northamptonshire Libraries wish to thank Mrs. Violet Sturgess and her daughter, Mrs. Mary Mustin, for making Arthur Sturgess' memoirs available for publication, and for help in the preparation of the printed text. Thanks also go to the following who have assisted in the publication; the Rev. J. C. Royds, Mrs. P. Marcham, Mrs. M. Ashby, Mrs. J. Currie and Mr. J. P. Mustin; and to Mr. L. S. Axe of Loddington, Mrs. M. Hawkes of Loddington, and Mr. J. H. Paul, Headmaster of Maidwell Hall School, for permission to publish their photographs.

INTRODUCTION

Arthur Sturgess moved to Loddington, near Kettering, in 1910 at the age of five. He describes his life there before and during the First World War. After a brief spell in Liverpool, he returned to Northamptonshire and became a successful builder in the Kettering area.

The original manuscript of 'A Northamptonshire Lad' was discovered by his daughter Mary after his death in 1979. Although a few minor alterations were unavoidable, the greater part has been left in Arthur Sturgess' own direct and effective style.

CHAPTER I
Early Days at Loddington

My first hazy recollections are of my elder brother George on the Doncaster racecourse. We had the lower half of a Woodbine Box and cut holes in each side. We passed string through the holes to make a large loop and this went over the head. The box was filled with Butter Scotch which we sold at $\frac{1}{2}$d per bar. I don't remember whether we made a profit or not — I was only five at the time.

The next thing I remember is being dressed in my Sunday best and told to behave, as we were going on a train journey. I can't recall any details of the journey except that my elder sister Alice put me on the carriage seat and told me to sit still. My feet didn't even reach the front edge of the seat. Then at last we arrived at our destination, Kettering. The place was a hive of activity. Smoke and steam filled the platform, porters and passengers with hand trucks and luggage were dashing about, and I was glad when we emerged from the front entrance. There were several horse carriages and carts waiting to pick up the passengers, when we were hailed by a woman with a pony and trap.

She told us her name was Mrs. Davenport and that she would convey us to Loddington. The pony didn't look very big to me, and I thought by the time we were all in the trap it would go up in the air. There were seven of us counting the baby, Mrs Davenport, mother carrying the baby, brother George, sister Alice, myself, sister Ruth, in that order, George being the oldest of the children.

It was the 16th October 1910, the day before my fifth birthday. Dad was a steam digger driver, working for the Staveley Iron and Coal Company. He had taken a job at Loddington Ironstone Company driving No. 1 digger. He had managed to get a house, and we were on our way to join him.

The trap was a back-to-back affair, four facing front and three facing back. With our hand luggage we made quite a load, and although I was quite sure the pony would suddenly go up in the air, Mrs. Davenport handled him with skill and managed to keep four feet on the ground.

It was a pleasant four-mile journey from Kettering station to the village. We were almost there and passed a row of cottages known as Three Chimneys when some small boys, about my own age, tried to jump on for a free ride. But Mrs. Davenport was equal to the occasion and using her whip to great effect they soon made off: not, however, before they had put up their fists to me and threatened what they would do when we next met.

When we arrived at our new home we discovered the furniture had not yet arrived, so one of the neighbours offered to put us up. Her name was Mrs. Chapman; she had a daughter about my age and we got on very well. The Chapmans did all they could to make us comfortable even if we did have to sleep five to a bed. It was only for two or three days: then we moved into the new house as soon as our furniture came.

I started school on the Monday after we arrived, and the first boy I saw was John Church, the boy who had put up his fist to me in the trap. It seems I, as a new boy, had to prove myself and in a few minutes we were locked in 'mortal combat'. Miss Wattam the Infants' teacher parted us. She proceeded to give me a good telling off and said if she caught me fighting again I should be sent before the Head Mistress for real punishment — all this before I even entered the School!

I saw John Church again at playtime and we soon became firm friends. It was a pleasant school, made up of three classes: Infants (Miss Wattam), juniors (Miss Buswell) and seniors (Mrs. Sharman — 'Dotty'). There was a playground in front for infants and girls; and at the back there was a large playground for boys.

I am afraid I was not a good scholar. I never paid attention to the lessons: my mind was full of other things, like making cat-a-pults, conker fighting, swapping knives etc.

With the help of John Church I soon got to know the inhabitants of the village. There were three farmers: Mr. J. Cook, Mr. Williams, and Mr. Broomhead. I soon became friendly with the Williams family: five daughters and two sons. Evelyn, the youngest daughter, was a few months younger than me, and we spent a lot of our spare time playing around the farm.

Mr. Davenport was the village baker: always very busy, too

much to do and not enough time. It was a family business: they were also the carriers and trap hire firm conveying the villagers to and from Kettering. There were seven in the family: Will, Madge, Norman, Grace and Silvia. Silvia was the youngest, I think she was about a year younger than me: she was the most beautiful girl I had ever seen. Platinum blond hair that always looked as if it had just been washed and brushed, it reached almost to her waist. She had a milk and roses complexion and a pleasant personality. I was ready to slay a dozen dragons just to see her smile. She was in the same class as me and I never missed an opportunity to render her a little service.

William Davenport, the village baker and carrier, with his wife, Elizabeth, and sons William and Norman.

The two-up, two-down cottage in Ellistown, Loddington, where the
Sturgess family lived.

George Johnson was the village butcher. He loved his beer, a
shilling on the horses, and cricket, in that order. His wife was a
typical butcher's wife, plump and jolly. They had three children,
two boys and one girl. They lived in the Manor House which stood
back from the street and they sold their meat from a little shop
in the front.

We lived at No. 2 Ellistown, a row of cottages owned by the
Staveley Company. Mother ruled the roost and was very proud of
her brood: woe betide anyone who laid a finger on any of us. She
was firm but kind and was always our refuge in times of trouble.
She was Welsh, born in Flintshire, the daughter of the local chapel
parson. On leaving school she went into domestic service, first as
a lady's companion, then children's nurse and chaperone. Dad was
born in Sherborne, Dorset, the son of the local butcher; but as
soon as he was old enough he made his way up to the industrial
North, eventually becoming a crane driver.

The Loddington Ironstone Mines had just installed their first
mechanical digger; he had secured the job of driver and the future

looked set fair. Although Dad's wage was a little above the average it was difficult for mother to make ends meet with a family of eight. Perhaps we were not the best dressed, but there was always plenty of good food available.

We were taught from a very early age to fend for ourselves. We had a fair-sized garden at the back of our house and a pig-sty that would hold up to four porkers. When the porkers were about six or seven stone, three were sold to the butcher while the other one was fed up to bacon weight for our own use, nine to ten stone. Butcher Johnson would come with all his tackle and do the killing. There were several families in the Row who kept pigs and when there was a killing we would all share in the offal; nothing was wasted except perhaps the squeal. This scheme worked very well and it meant every month or so we should get our share of offal. With our own pig the flitches and hams were salted and hung up for curing: this ensured our supply of bacon and ham.

We had wire netting around the garden and kept about half a dozen hens, just for our own needs. Vegetables were plentiful and cheap so we had to buy these from the neighbours until we were old enough to grow our own. Rabbits were a good additional supply of food at about 4d to 6d each. It seemed to me the main interest in life was food, how to obtain it, how to store it, how to cook it. My chief interest was eating it!

We were a happy family. In the winter evenings we had to find our own amusement. There would be the usual flare-up when six children were playing together but mother soon put a stop to that – her word was law. Dad never said anything. They were happy days and when I look back I am amazed how well we got on. Mother used to put bricks in the oven; wrapped in flannel and put in each bed they made very good hot water bottles. When we first moved in we had only candles for lighting, but as soon as possible we went over to paraffin: a lamp was fixed to the ceiling for safety. This was a big improvement but a couple of years later when we went on to electricity we thought this was the height of luxury, you just press a switch and a light comes on. It was the talking point in the village for some time.

We had two water supplies. One was pumped from the brook by windmill: this fed the tap at the sink but it had to be boiled before drinking. The other was from the pump in the yard; this was fed by a spring — it was always cool, crystal clear, and safe to drink.

We got on well with the neighbours and although there was an open yard along the back of the Row, there was seldom a quarrel.

For me there was only one fly in the ointment; his name was Frank Johnson. He was about a year older, and bigger than me. We had the usual fights and they all finished in a tie. I never sought his company but he always found me. He spelled trouble every time. He loved to open the pig-sty gates and let the pigs loose on the gardens, then run off quickly to tell the owner it was Arthur Sturgess. I would then let all the hens out and say it was Frank Johnson.

We had only just settled in the village when we were invited to a tea party in Broomhead's barn. This was to celebrate the coronation of King George V. The barn was nice and clean, decorated with bunting and flags etc. Trestle tables were well laden with the usual jellies, fresh cream and a nice selection of fancy cakes etc. and after a good tuck-in we had the usual games. When it was time to leave we all got into a line and went out of the front door single file past Mrs. Howard the parson's wife, and Miss Broomhead the farmer's sister. They had two tea chests by the door and each child received an apple, an orange, and a present from the tea chest. To my astonishment and joy I was given a 'pocket knife' by Miss Broomhead. This was just about the greatest day of my life, and as I was walking away with my new treasure, Mrs. Howard called 'Come back, boy', and taking away my new knife she remarked: 'He's much too young for a knife. Here, this is more suitable' and she gave me a purse. To add insult to injury it was a lady's purse. I never forgave Mrs. Howard for that.

The next three years seemed to slip away very quickly. We spent most of our time out of doors. In the winter it was the usual things, snowballing and sliding; there were always some good ponds in the ironstone pits where we could skate and slide. Of course the summer was best, especially the long school holidays. We were allowed to wander through the fields gathering wild flowers, providing we didn't disturb the animals. On our return to school there was always a prize for the best bunch of wild flowers.

It would be 1913, summer, when the County Council decided to make the road from Cransley to Loddington. There seemed to be hundreds of men, horses and carts, and big steam rollers. Two horses pulled the water cart, which was filled from the stream at the bottom of the hill. I was in my element helping the men on this job. I would be lifted on to the front horse and I would ride down to the stream, help to pump the tank full, then ride back to the site. There was a handle at the side of the cart: if you pulled it hard enough it would throw out a spray of water right across the road. I had some fun with this.

We always had a good time in the harvest fields. Armed with stout sticks we stood around the edge of the corn and got the rabbits as they made a dash for freedom. All the rabbits were placed in a heap and when the cutting was finished the farmer would share them out to the helpers. I often had one, sometimes two and this, of course, added to the pleasure.

One place in the village which always attracted the children was the Blacksmith's Shop.

> Under the spreading chestnut tree
>   the village Smithy stands,
> The muscles on his brawny arms
>   stood out like iron bands.

I am afraid our blacksmith was not at all like that. Mr. Wheatley was about average height but always looked ill, very thin and pale. He left most of the heavy work till the evening when the older boys would give him a hand. I always loved to watch the glow from his fire, and the cloud of smoke that came from fitting the hot shoe to the horses' hoofs. Sometimes, if a horse was a bit troublesome, he would get me to stand by its head to try to soothe it while the shoeing was going on. I was introduced to horses at a very early age and saw nothing to fear in them although some of them were very big Shires.

Saturday was always a good day for me. I used to take Dad's breakfast and as it was a short day I was allowed to stay. I always had old clothes on for this and spent the time climbing all over the machines, helping to stoke the fire, and going around with a waste cloth and oil can. It was a very large digger with a scoop bucket that cleared the earth covering the ironstone. Dad was up front working the levers; I spent my time at the back with the fireman, Jack Penn, keeping up a head of steam to drive the machine. Jack taught me how to work the 'injector' which transferred the water

Mr. Wheatley, the blacksmith (third from left), outside the forge at Loddington, about 1914.

from the tank to the boiler. This made me feel very important and I always went home very black but very happy.

The ironstone now uncovered was loaded into iron trucks by hand; the men on this job being known as 'hand fillers'. When the trucks were full, they were towed away by a small engine to the docks, where they were emptied into the larger L.M.S. wagons and then on to the furnaces. Two of the small engines we called 'Locos': Peter Cook and Tom Sawford were the drivers. Each had a 'runner', a man to couple up the trucks, and you can imagine what a time I had there. I knew both drivers well and was allowed to ride with them on the footplate. I was soon turning on the hand-brake or opening the 'regulators' to the drivers' instructions, and to make my heaven complete, Frank Johnson was not allowed anywhere near the diggers or the locos.

In the winter another occupation I always looked forward to was thrashing time on the farms. Mr. Cook owned the equipment, consisting of a steam traction engine and drum. The sheaves of corn were fed into this to be separated: corn out the back, chaff and shavings from the side, and the straw out the front on to the elevator – an endless belt conveying the straw to be stacked. There was always a lot of men, steam and fun getting the equipment into position. It was the one occasion when the farmers welcomed children. Rats and mice made their homes in the corn stacks so a fence of wire netting was erected round each stack and when thrashing started we all stood round with thatch pegs and killed them as they tried to make their escape. It was a good opportunity for the farmers to get rid of the vermin.

Mr. Adam Steel was the squire of the village and he lived in the Hall. The family consisted of three daughters and two sons, all of them grown up: the sons were in the Army while the daughters lived at home. Two of them were regular members of the local hunt. The hounds often met at the Hall and we would be given an hour off from school for the occasion. I used the 'Meet' to admire the horses: there would be some lovely animals, well groomed and frisky, with their coats glistening in the sun, and as they rode away I vowed that one day I would ride one . . . .

Mr. Steel was a tall, grey-haired man with a Van Dyke beard and a humorous twinkle in his eyes, but ill health kept him indoors. Nelli, the eldest daughter, was away most of the time; Miss Camila

(Lil) and Miss Mary stayed at home with father. I don't know how many staff they employed but there seemed to be a good team of grooms, gardeners, cowmen, farmhands and a full domestic staff supervised by the Housekeeper.

About this time George Johnson, the butcher, being unable to make his business pay, sold up and took one of the estate cottages. Mrs. Johnson became Cook at the Hall and George was given a job on the farm. I went around quite often with their two sons, George and Herbert: both turned out to be good cricketers, like their father. I had many a free meal with them, sitting at a big deal table in the Hall kitchen. I remember in particular the large mugs of cocoa made with milk fresh from the Jersey cows.

Our church was set in pleasant surroundings opposite the village green. The Rev. T. B. Howard officiated, with his wife assisting on the organ. I was soon to don a surplice and with my hands and face scrubbed until they shone, joined the rest of the Gang in the choir. "Onward Christian Soldiers", "Fight the Good Fight" — I liked the singing and joined in whole-heartedly, especially at Harvest Thanksgiving and for Easter carols. The Rector however was an old man: his sermons were long and boring and it was then that trouble started in the choir stalls. The churchwarden would threaten to throw us all out if we didn't sit still.

The Chapel was more to our liking: a small building in the centre of the village opposite the *New Inn*. It was a Congregational chapel and preachers from Rothwell came to take the service every Sunday evening. A harmonium provided the music. The atmosphere was more friendly than at the church: our Gang was often threatened but never actually thrown out.

In the summer time the church and the chapel took the children on an outing. When an outing was due, we made sure we attended often enough to qualify and thus enjoyed the best of both worlds. We were taken by wagonette drawn by two horses to a place of interest and perhaps a picnic tea. I went mainly for the ride and made sure I got a seat up front where I could see the horses.

We had our usual supply of visitors. My favourite was 'Piccolo Pete' who called two or three times during the summer. He used to play a 'penny whistle' and as he approached the village we would run out to meet him and follow him around like the Pied Piper of Hamelin. This was good business for him as we would all

Loddington Church.

Mawsley House on the right, with Loddington Chapel in the background.

run home to get a penny for the Tin Whistle Man. He used to play the overture from 'William Tell', 'Poet and Peasant', 'In a monastery garden', – all good stuff. He was a great artist and we were always sorry to see him go.

Then there was the Umbrella Man. He had a hand truck and would repair a damaged umbrella while you waited. He didn't talk much but it was fascinating to watch.

The comedian of the lot was the Old Clothes Man. He carried a sack full of second-hand clothes and he would take out an old waistcoat, a jacket and a pair of trousers and then he would dance round in a circle rendering a monologue as he put the garments on, ending with a few verses from Shakespeare. He would pull the most awful faces and his antics would have us rolling with laughter. He never failed to attract a crowd and seemed to do a fair trade.

'Knives to grind and scissors to mend' was the call of one old boy. He had what looked like a wheelbarrow frame on which there was a large grindstone with a treadle attached and of course, we had to have a go on the treadle while he sharpened the knives and scissors.

Perhaps the cleverest of them all was the travelling Tinker. He could make anything or mend anything, leaking kettles, saucepans etc. I never saw him do it but he claimed he could put copper bottoms on aluminium kettles and aluminium bottoms on copper kettles. He loved to tell about the old lady who asked him: 'Are you putting a copper bottom on that, my man?' The answer was: 'No, Mum: I'm aluminium bottoming it.' It was always a good laugh when we tried to say that quickly.

During the summer months we were favoured with the presence of two characters we called 'Old Posh' and 'Hip-my-Haddie'. They were just like Laurel and Hardy; the fat one always wore a bowler hat and the thin one a flat cap. They did casual work on the local farms. They would be up early in the morning, work hard till noon, get a sub from the farmer and then off to the pub. The afternoon would be spent under a shady tree, and with their tongues well loosened with good ale they would tell us the most far-fetched stories about the heroic deeds they had performed on the battle fields. They claimed to be old soldiers, and told us about their adventures overseas and their fights with Red Indians. We sat around with our mouths open, taking it all in; but they were quite harmless, very friendly men.

We never heard of a child being molested, there was no vandalism, no violence, and the only noise came from the birds. The sky was for the skylark, the meadows for the animals, the roads for horses and carts. There were no aeroplanes, no motors or tractors to shatter the tranquillity of 1913 and peace prevailed.

The Hargrave family ran the Grange farm, half way between Loddington and Cransley. The youngest son, William, attended our School. He was about my age and I often spent a day with him on the farm. Mr. Hargrave let it be known that he would pay fourpence per hour for turnip pullers. Our Gang, always on the look-out for a 'fast buck', decided to have a go. Eight of us including brother George turned up early on the Saturday morning: Mr. Hargraves took us to the field and after giving us our instructions he left, saying he would be back later in the afternoon. It turned out to be a cold, wet job. We had had enough long before knocking-off time but we stuck to our task bravely till dusk, and as the Boss didn't turn up we decided to go up to the house to wait for him.

Some of the Gang thought fourpence was not enough and they started talking about sixpence so, after some discussion, we agreed to ask for sixpence. All we needed now was a spokesman and Arthur Sturgess was elected after a show of hands. They reasoned that as I knew the family I was the best man for the job. I protested, but it was pointed out that I had been elected by an overwhelming majority, so I agreed.

Mrs. Hargrave met us at the door. She told us the Boss was not back yet but we could wait in the kitchen. She made a large jug of tea and brought out a plate of cakes to help us while away the time. We had just finished our snack when the Boss came in, apologised for keeping us waiting, and said he would pay us right away. A good dig in my back from brother George brought me to the fore. I said: 'Mr. Hargrave.' 'Yes, Artie, what is it?' 'We have worked well to-day.' 'Yes, Artie, I noticed as I came in.' 'Mr. Hargrave, er . . . um . . . er – do you think you could make it sixpence an hour?"

I have never seen a man laugh so much in my life and when he had finished he patted me on the head and said: 'All right, Oliver, sixpence it shall be.' I couldn't understand the 'Oliver' bit, not having read any of Charles Dickens at that time, but we all went

home happy in the knowledge that we had gained 50% increase
in our pay.

One afternoon as I left school with Johnson at my heels, we
saw the thrashing tackle making its way to Steel's stackyard, and
of course, we had to be in there. We watched at a discreet distance
as the men manoeuvred the drum and elevator into position; then
the engine had to be carefully set into line, with wood blocks
against the wheels to keep it steady. All this done it was too late
to start thrashing that day, so Jim Tilly, the driver, damped down
his fire and placed a slate on the chimney with a brick to hold it
down. When the men had all gone, Johnson said: 'Let's see if we
can start the engine!' I had a funny feeling in my stomach that
we were heading for trouble, but with Johnson prompting me and
being anxious to show off my skill, I agreed to have a go. Climbing
on to the engine, I noticed there was enough steam in the boiler
to get a start. I pulled open the regulator and immediately the
slate with the brick on it shot about 20 feet into the air and the
old engine went 'puff, puff.' We knocked the blocks away from
the wheels, pushed the lever into the forward position, and as
Johnson pulled the cord to blow the whistle we were away.
Another pull on the regulator told me we were getting short of
steam but as we debated what to do about it, a loud voice called
'Hi, what the ****** are you up to?'

We shot off at speed and did a two-field detour back to our
home. Next day the news didn't leak out — it shot around the
village like wildfire. It seems the shortage of steam saved us from
dire punishment, perhaps imprisonment for life. The farmer came
around to our house next evening and gave me a very uncom-
fortable half hour.

The spring of 1914 came in early and warm. I loved to wander
around the fields on my own, with my cat-a-pult and pocket full
of pebbles. When the Gang were there they made so much noise
they frightened everything away. There was one hedge with plenty
of rabbit holes which I loved to stalk; when all was quiet the
rabbits would come out to feed. My idea was to wait quietly until
they had worked their way out into the field, and then let fly with
my cat-a-pult.

One lovely warm day when the hedges were in full bloom with
dog daisies and honeysuckle, the grass was already long, and the

Loddington School.

only sound was from the bees, I was on all fours creeping stealthily along the side of the hedge when I came to a small bush. I was about to creep round the bush when I saw him about three feet away, his eyes fixing me with a cold, unblinking stare. He had a long face with a black, twitching nose: two rows of white teeth shone in the sunlight and saliva dripped from his lower jaw. I was rooted to the spot. I must have blinked, and he was gone without a sound – a beautiful, big male fox and after my rabbit indeed . . .

And so we carried on with our many activities: riding on the locos, climbing about the diggers (another one had arrived, by the way, giving me another interest), attending chapel and church, helping on the farms, and looking forward to the summer holidays. Then for the first time I heard talk of a war. It didn't bother us, we were fully occupied with other things; but then when we were about half through the harvest, it came – we were at war with Germany.

It didn't have any immediate effect and we were back at school before we noticed that the young men of the village were joining the Army. Recruiting posters were stuck up and the Squire offered a horse to any of his grooms who joined the cavalry. I think about half a dozen joined up, and after their initial training they were issued with a uniform and they came to collect their horses. The morning of their departure, all the children were paraded in front of the School and we sang 'Rule, Britannia' and cheered as they cantered off down the street, but I don't think any returned.

By 1915 everyone was saying the war would soon be over, but already the Zeppelins had dropped bombs on London, where there were no aerial defences. Untrained men were being sent to France and German battleships had shelled coastal towns such as Bridlington where several people were killed. It seemed that England was quite unprepared for war.

Lord Kitchener appealed for more recruits and we learned recruiting songs like

> 'We don't want to lose you
>   but we think you ought to go,
> Your King and your Country
>   both need you so.'

And

'Go and put your khaki on,
    Wear it like a man;
Follow those who led the way
    Since the war began.
You are wanted at the front,
    There is work for you;
Leave your football,
Leave your golf,
And see old England through.'

The newspaper headlines told of our merchant ships being sunk by German U-boats, but Lloyd George started the convoy system, against strong opposition, and he proved to be right. The losses were cut to about 1%. We read about the Battle of the Somme: about 20,000 killed in one day, with a total of 57,000 casualties.

The wounded soldiers were already returning from the war. Two brothers I knew well joined up at the outbreak of war: Bill and Jack Sawford. Bill was killed in action and Jack lost his arm. News came through of many more who would never return. In school we sang

'Oh, God of love
Oh, King of Peace
Make wars throughout
the world cease!'

And

'O hear us when we cry to thee
    for those in peril on the sea.'

Jack Sawford was one of the first wounded soldiers to come home from the war. After a period of convalescence he started to work for farmer Williams, although he now only had one arm. He soon became proficient with an artificial one and a hook. One day I went with him to fetch a load of swedes from the field. These had to be pulled, the tops and bottoms cut off, and loaded into the cart. We used an old but sharp dinner knife to cut the tops and when I had a go the knife slipped up and made a cut in my thumb. Seeing by the amount of blood that the cut could be fairly deep, he wrapped his handkerchief round it and we both ran to the village. The blacksmith came to our aid. After washing the wound with Jeyes Fluid he applied a bandage and advised me to see a doctor at once. I had to stand around for about two hours before the surgery opened; then, being first in, the doctor looked at my bandaged thumb and told me it would be better to leave it as it was! He would call on Sunday morning while he was on his rounds. It was quite dark by the time I got home, tired and feeling very sorry for myself. I still have the scar.

That was a bad winter. It seemed as though we were under a heavy black cloud – but worse was to come. A diptheria epidemic swept the country, and as there was no vaccine many thousands of children died. We had our share, and there were many vacant places in our classroom. One day, Grace Davenport told the teacher that Silvia was not well and would not be able to attend school. We said prayers every day for the sick but Silvia died about a week later. My little friend with the silver hair became a victim of the dreadful disease.

The sinking of the 'Lusitania' did nothing to boost morale, and many more such losses were to follow. In 1916, women were recruited to work in the factories, and a new Factory Act brought in fresh safety rules and regulations. Children were compelled to stay at school until they were thirteen years of age. Wages began to rise. The Old Age Pension, introduced by Lloyd George, was increased. Income tax, too, went up from one shilling and three-pence to two shillings and sixpence. Paper money took the place of the gold sovereign.

Lloyd George became the first Welsh Prime Minister. The German battleship 'Emden' was sunk by the Australian cruiser 'Sydney'. The Battle of Jutland was short and sharp: the German fleet turned tail but British losses were greater than the German. So it went on. We had no radio, of course, but relied on the newspapers and rumour. Lord Kitchener was drowned on his way to Russia.

In spite of all this life had to go on in our village. An Entertainment Committee was formed and soon got to work organising concerts and dances. All services and refreshments were given free but any profit went into the 'Comforts Fund' for the soldiers; and nearly everyone took part. The artists were all volunteers and we got many a good laugh at their efforts. It was all good fun and took people's minds off the war. It also provided many parcels for the village chaps away fighting the war.

Major Brookshanks and his wife took up residence in the White House. He had retired from the Army after many years' service abroad. He looked the part: average height, slim build, clipped moustache, and a pleasant enough chap when you got to know him. When he had settled in, he announced that he would like to start a Boy Scout Troop at Loddington and so in due course the 1st Peewit Patrol was launched. He owned a large touring car and would take us to all the Scout Jamborees, carnivals and garden parties etc. We bought our uniforms on the instalment plan, and though 'I say it who shouldn't', we looked quite smart.

The Major would throw a rope over the branch of a tree and we had to climb it (this just suited me). He had a scaffold pole of two trestles and we learned knot tying — half hitch, clove hitch, sheepshank, sheepbend etc. — all good fun in the summer. In the winter evenings we all gathered in the kitchen and listened with our mouths open as he read aloud such stores as 'Robinson Crusoe' and 'Treasure Island.' We were sworn in after we had learned the Boy Scout Code of Honour and from then on we were on the lookout for some old lady to escort across the street. But there was no traffic in our village except perhaps a solitary duck making its way back to the farmyard — very frustrating . . . The Daylight Saving Bill was passed. We spent our extra hours learning the Morse Code and Semaphore.

By 1917 the war effort was going well at home. Everyone was going flat out but wages were going up far beyond the cost of living. We were encouraged to help with food production on the farms and allotments. That summer, women and children worked harder than ever with the haytime, harvest, and even root crops. I landed a contract with farmer Williams to take the cows out to the fields every morning and bring them back for milking each evening. It was 10 o'clock by the time I got to school and I had to leave an hour early in the afternoon. This played havoc with my schooling but it brought in two shillings per week.

Mr. Williams was a dairy farmer and had a herd of about 35–40 cows. A herd of this size needed quite a lot of pasture and when the summer holidays started I had to keep them grazing on the grass verge at the side of the road all day — a lonely and boring job but it saved the regular pastures. I had no watch. The only traffic was an occasional horse and cart. I took sandwiches and a bottle of cold tea. I always had an empty corn sack with me which was to keep me dry when it rained, or to spread on the bank to sit on if the grass was damp.

I tried to pass the time away with my cat-a-pult, plaiting corn, and making wooden whistles. Sometimes one of the Gang would come with me. Frank Johnson was coming until I told him the bull ran with the herd, then he suddenly remembered a very pressing appointment. The leader of the herd was a large Red Poll called Tarry. She gave the most milk and had that superior air. She didn't need a watch for she could be relied on to lead the others back for milking dead on time. They all had names and their own stand in the milking shed. It was my job there to fix a chain round the neck of each cow and then I could go home. I could manage this all right with the cows, but the bull's neck was too fat and I couldn't get my arms around to fix the chain. After several attempts we decided it would be best if we ignored each other: he would go his way and I would go mine.

The Johnson family went to live at Draughton. This was good news for many people.

One day there were many storm clouds and distant rumbles of thunder and as the day wore on it started to rain. Taking up my corn sack I found a well-sheltered spot in the hedge, made myself comfortable, and waited for the storm. Suddenly I awoke. I had no idea how long I had been asleep. The rain had stopped and I didn't like the quietness. Looking out, I could see the road was nearly dry but there wasn't a cow in sight. I dashed off in the direction of the village and was just in time to see the last cow entering the farmyard. Tarry had taken them home on time and no one knew I had had a nap. Tarry took no notice of the new 'summer time' arrangements; it was milking time when *she* was ready.

Ration books were introduced. It seemed there was plenty of food in the country for the present, but the ration books were the fairest way to distribute it. The war news was gloomy: people were still talking about the Russian Revolution, and our soldiers were fighting in the Passchendale mud.

About two days before my 12th birthday, after supper, farmer

Cook called. He was talking to my parents in the front room for some time. Then I was called in and told I was about to play a bigger part in the war effort: I was to work full-time for Mr. Cook. It seems a new Act had been passed allowing boys of 12 years to work on the farm full-time for the duration of the war. If, however, the war was over before I was thirteen years old, I would have to go back to school. All this was a sudden and complete surprise to me. I told Mrs. Sharman I was leaving school: she tut-tutted a bit — a lot in fact.

It was easy to find another boy to take the cows to the field and before I had had time to think things out I was being called at 6 o'clock and with my lunch basket packed I was off to start my first day.

Ern Wilson was assistant horsekeeper to his father George ('Mugs' we called him) and I was to work with Ern. He explained that we were going to plough in the big field, using three horses to pull a two-furrow plough. My job was to keep the horses going and lead the front horse around when we came to the headland. The horses on the Williams farm were what we called 'half-legged' — smaller, more manoeuvrable, ideal for doing jobs around the farm — but Cook's horses were giants. They were top-class shires, slow but very strong: they would work all day on the heavy land and pull enormous loads.

Daylight was breaking through a heavy mist as we entered the field. It didn't take long to hook up to the plough, and we were away. It was a large field, about 40 acres, and seemed miles to the other end. Once down and back was called a 'bought'. The topsoil was damp and stuck to my boots and soon I was carrying two to three pounds of soil on each foot. I made frequent stops to move it, but it soon built up again.

I was glad of the first break: lunchtime, 9.30. After half an hour we were off again, due to work till 2 o'clock. The soil got heavier on my boots and by 12 noon I was about all in. Ern Wilson was a kindly man and wanted to help but he had a job to do — to keep ploughing. However, when we got back to the headland, he suggested he would do a 'bought' on his own while I rested on my sack in the hedge. By the time he got back my rest had done me good so I had another go; but by 1.30 I could go no further. Ern told me he would have to do another 'bought'. My head was spinning as I flopped down on my sack, and in about ten seconds I was fast asleep.

The next thing I knew was Ern lifting me up and saying, 'Come on, boy, we're going home.' He put me on the front horse and we rode back to the farm. After a good meal, and with the soil off my boots, I went back to help in the stables: mucking-out, carrying in fresh bedding, cutting chaff. This kept us busy till 5.30, then back home to supper. Mother advised an early night, as I had to be up early in the morning. As my head touched the pillow, the words of a hymn came to my mind: 'The day thou gavest, Lord, is ended . . . '

I well remember the next day. There was no fog, a gentle breeze was blowing, and this dried the topsoil that no longer clung to my boots so life was much easier. I was always ready for lunchtime. Dad used to fry a thick slice of ham, cut the top of a cottage loaf in half, fry the two halves in the fat till they were golden brown, and with the thick home-cured ham I had a substantial sandwich. I never left a bit, not even a crumb for the birds for I was a growing lad.

The harrowing and drilling followed the ploughing. As cold rain cut my face, my mind would go back to school and the big stove sending a warm glow round the classroom.

It was 1918 and Spring at last. My spirits rose as the birds began to sing and set about their task of house building and starting a family. Soon we were busy haymaking and preparing for the harvest. There is always plenty to do on a farm.

The sight of the grooms exercising the hunters was quite a common one. They had a stable boy named Dick Cox. How I envied him! 'That's the job I'd like — and I bet I could ride better than him!'

The football club and the cricket club were a joint concern. Boys were not allowed to join until they were 14 years of age but an exception was made in my case because I was a full-time worker. I loved both games, but football was my favourite. Most of the young chaps were in the army, so I soon got a place in both teams. I had the distinction also of being the smallest player. The cricket field was pleasantly situated in front of the church and when the team played at home it was quite an occasion. The players' wives and mothers would prepare refreshments for the visitors, and these were set out on trestle tables. Tea was taken when the first side was out. There was always a barrel of beer to make it even more worth-while. On a fine day, the villagers would turn out in good numbers to watch the match.

The war news was not good: we were still reading about the losses on land and sea. The Americans had been in the war for some time but they had not yet made much impact. There was more trouble in Ireland with the Black-and-Tans. The British government were falling out over the best way to use the R.A.F. The only good news was the extension of the national insurance scheme, with increased benefits to cover all workers earning under £5 per week. By August, the newspapers were talking about a strong rumour that the Germans were asking for an Armistice but nobody believed this, of course, and the rumour persisted.

P.C. Hughes was responsible for law and order in the village, and although he was near to retiring age he could still do a good sprint. He deceived me on many occasions and I felt the might of his cane across my backside — 'Instant Justice', he called it.

When the corn drilling was finished, we were preparing a field for root crops and P.C. Hughes, now retired, came to work on our farm as a part-time labourer. He was working on the same field and we became firm friends, my misdeeds forgotten. One day he called me over to look at his latest purchase: a new invention called a Thermos Flask. He poured me a tot of steaming hot tea and we talked about the wonders of science.

The harvest was in and we were getting well into September. I knew that the ploughing would soon begin again and this caused me some concern. I did not like the thought of walking up and down that big field again, but I was trapped: it was either the plough or school till my birthday in October.

CHAPTER II
In the Stables

Then it happened. I heard the Cox family were leaving the village. That evening sharp after supper I called on the head groom, Mr. Jack Townsend. I explained I was interested in the stable boy's job but I was tied to the farm until I was thirteen. I knew the Townsends very well: they had a son Fred who was in our Gang. Mr. Townsend said he thought I would be very suitable but he would have to see Miss Camila. In due course I was summoned to the Hall and after a pleasant chat Miss Camila told me I could have the job and they would hold it open until my birthday. This was wonderful news and I lost no time in telling Mr. Cook I should be leaving to work in the hunting stables. Mother raised no objections as the new job would bring in fourteen shillings a week — a four-shillings increase.

I had always fancied myself as a bit of a whistler and now I exercised that talent to the full. I didn't know many tunes apart from hymns, so I blew my teeth out on the William Tell overture, 'In a monastery garden', or 'Poet and Peasant' — tunes I had learned from 'Piccolo Pete'.

On 17th October, 1918 I said goodbye to Ern Wilson and Mr. Cook. He didn't take it very well but I promised to go back to him if I didn't like it in the stables. The war was still on but I was now 13 years old and free to work where I liked.

Work in the stables started at 6.30 a.m. I was there by 6 o'clock. I had on a pair of cavalry twill riding breeches and khaki puttees and with my hair brushed well back and boots highly polished I was ready for action. I soon fell into the stable routine. Jack Townsend was head groom; Bob Holman — a thin, rather nervous chap about 35 years old — was second in command. We had four hunters and a carriage horse to look after. The two daughters, Miss Camila and Miss Mary, hunted about three days a week. Sometimes they would have a second horse and that meant one

Loddington Hall, the home of Mr. Adam Steel and his family.

of the grooms would take a fresh horse to an agreed point and bring the tired horse back. It was a busy job but the work was much lighter than the farm. We always had a 'siesta' in the afternoons when the men would wash and shave and then put their feet up for about half an hour. I would take this opportunity to pop into the kitchen to see if I could give Mrs. Johnson a hand and my reward would be a large mug of tea and a sizeable chunk of rice cake. I got to know the servants quite well and they invited me to join them at their dancing classes which were held once a week in the servants' hall. This was a laugh.

They danced to a very primitive music box. You had to insert a sheet of thick brown paper with a lot of holes punched in it: it was then only a matter of turning the handle. I soon realised why I had been invited: it was a tiring job on the handle but if you stopped, the music stopped. We were supposed to take turns, but when I called for a relief they were all deaf. This called for more direct action. I selected a waltz then starting slowly, increased the speed until the dancers were going madly round the room. They all finished up in a heap on the floor. I had a rough five minutes after that, but they got the message and I was able to get in some dancing.

I started my riding lessons on 'Old Bill', the carriage horse. This was a good arrangement, as he needed the exercise and I the experience. Townsend shortened the stirrups and found me a small saddle. 'Old Bill' was an easy old horse to handle and we got on well together. After a couple of weeks I was promoted to one of the hunters, a chestnut mare, and as there was no hunting that day we all went out together. This was a proud day for me. I felt on top of the world and listened carefully to Townsend's instructions:

. . . . 'Keep your head up, your hands down, your back straight, your knees in. Hold the reins firm, but not tight. Keep your mind on the job.'

We had travelled about two miles from the village and I was thinking there was nothing to it when, without warning, a cock pheasant flew up almost under my horse's feet. The mare gave a frightened snort and we were away. Townsend shouted, 'Hang on, Artie!' and I caught a glimpse of Bob Holman's startled face as I flashed past. As I could think of nothing better to do, I took Townsend's advice and hung on to the reins, but the mare had the bit between her teeth and although I pulled with all my strength, I made no impression. We were going at a terrific gallop, and I thought at least even Dick Turpin couldn't catch us at this speed. Some girls going to work called out, 'Steady, Artie, put the brake on.' We were galloping on the grass verge at the side of the road and after about a mile at top speed the mare began to slow down. A sharp pull on the reins brought the bit back into her mouth and I was in control.

I turned her around and trotted back to join up with the others, thinking: 'That's your lot, my boy: you've just had two rides, your first and your last, and you'll be lucky if you don't get the sack.' When we got within talking distance, Townsend called, 'Well done, Artie! You rode her well, boy.'

After that I was a regular rider at morning exercise. I was enjoying life to the full. Every morning, soon after 6 o'clock, I would walk up the village street whistling as loudly as I could. I learned years later that a wife would call to her husband: 'Come on, get up! Arthur Sturgess has gone by.' They didn't need an alarm clock.

The Steels owned several fields at Foxhall, about two miles away. One morning, Fred Skinner, the cowman, asked Townsend if I could be spared to give him a hand to move some young cattle from the home pastures to the Foxhall field. Townsend said, 'Go with him, Artie; the hounds meet at Foxhall today at 11 o'clock and you needn't hurry back.'

It was November 11th, 1918. We put the cattle in the field and arrived at the Foxhall Inn just before 11 o'clock. Some of the followers and horsemen had already gathered in front of the pub. The ironstone workers were busy in the pits opposite the pub, and Binky Binder, the foreman, was standing by the door of his office — which was a wooden shed connected to the Company's office by telephone. Drinks were strictly rationed and Tod Slow, the landlord, would only serve one half pint of beer to each customer. By now the hounds had arrived and the huntsman, having already had his drink, was ready to blow his horn for the 'Off', when Binky Binder came running and shouting as he waved his bowler hat: 'It's ALL OVER, IT'S ALL OVER, JUST HAD A MESSAGE ON THE PHONE, THE WAR'S *OVER*!'

The news spread like wildfire. Men appeared from nowhere. The horsemen dismounted and everyone went around back-slapping and shaking hands. Tod Slow suddenly appeared carrying two large milk pails full of beer; his wife followed with cups, mugs and glasses. 'Help yoursleves,' cried Tod, 'It's on the house!' I grabbed an enamel mug and dipped in. Tod kept the pails well topped up and about two hours later, the huntsmen, having forgotten about the Meet, were trying to help each other to mount. We had a good laugh at their efforts. Some decided to walk and lead their horses home.

Fred Skinner and I had plenty of jovial company on our journey back to Loddington. When we arrived, we were met by a large party of women and children all banging tin cans, and singing and dancing in the street. German prisoners working in the pits close by had joined them: with the war over, they were no longer enemies but friends!

The newspapers gave details of the Armistice, the abdication of Kaiser Wilhelm from Germany and the continuing trouble in

Ireland. The winter of 1918–19 was a bad one: apart from the weather, the whole country was struck with the great influenza epidemic. 150,000 people died in this and we had our share. This time it took people of all ages: there were many new graves in the churchyard and many empty desks in the School. My sister Ruth, two years younger than me, had the scarlet fever it was only mother's careful nursing that saved her — she never left her side day or night.

In spite of all this, I carried on, engrossed in my work. I never missed a dancing class or a chunk of Mrs. Johnson's cake.

Young hunters are handled from birth; that is, as soon as they can walk. A small rope halter is put on their head and they are led around following their mother at exercise. When they are one year old ('yearlings') they are brought in from the fields to be trained for hunting. Townsend was a good man for this job. His approach was slow and careful: he was very patient and never lost his temper. Being a lightweight, it was my task to get the young horse used to having a rider. This was exciting. I got quite a few bruises before I learned how to land after being 'thrown' but it was a great feeling, after a few months, to ride a young horse out with the others at exercise.

But, as the saying goes, all good things must come to an end. Miss Mary Steel announced that she was going abroad, to Africa, to do missionary work. Miss Mary and my sister Alice, two years older than me, were good friends and she tried hard to get Alice to join her on the African venture. Alice was by this time an established machinist in a Kettering clothing factory, and after much careful thought she decided to stay put. With the hunting season now over, the horses were put out to grass. Bob Holman left to take a job at Kelmarsh, a neighbouring village; Jack Townsend went to work on the Hall farm; and I was transferred to the gardens and the house. We had a small pony for pulling the lawn mower: he was fitted out with boots made of leather with flat soles to prevent his shoes marking the lawn. My job was to lead him up and down while the gardener controlled the machine.

At the house I had many duties including stoking up all the fires with coal and logs. Next to the kitchen was the bakehouse, with a large, old-fashioned brick oven. I would light a fire in this, stoke it up with faggots until it was white hot, then rake out all the ashes;

the oven was then filled with bread tins which Mrs. Johnson had standing by. In due course the bread was taken out and the lovely brown loaves would be knocked out on to a large table to cool. It was very nice bread and Mrs. Johnson would give me a load to take home.

My wages were 14 shillings per week and when John Church told me he could get me a job at 25 shillings per week in engineering, I was very interested. I started the new job as soon as I had served my week's notice. It was in a small firm making ball bearings for Rover cars, and I was put to work on a drilling machine. I didn't like the indoor work, or the constant supervision and the monotony of the same job day after day, so I was not sorry when, after about three months, we were told the firm was closing down. At home, the harvest had been gathered in but I was confident I would soon be able to get work on the farms. I was prepared to do anything, except ploughing.

It was only a few days later I spied a stranger approaching. I guessed he was just turned forty, about 5 feet 10, with a small moustache and a pleasant face. He carried a small attaché case and to complete the outfit had a raincoat over one shoulder. He asked me quite a lot of questions: was I local, was there a pub in the village where he could get lodgings etc. He told me he worked for the Forestry Commission and needed some men to plant trees behind the ironstone workings. I gave him all the information he wanted as we walked back to the New Inn. Jack Rippin, the landlord, could provide lodgings, so after further conversation when I explained how lucky he was to make my acquaintance just when I happened to be available, he engaged me on the spot as foreman at £2.10s. per week, starting the next day. I couldn't believe it, and when I told the family they couldn't believe it either.

I met my new friend the next day (I shall refer to him as the Manager as I have forgotten his name) and took him to the site where the trees were to be planted. He told me the trees were at Kettering station and I was to arrange transport to get them to the site. Farmer Cook obliged with a waggon and two horses, and with Ern Wilson as my mate we collected the trees while the Manager went to Desborough Labour Exchange to arrange for a dozen men. The men were to start in two days, so that gave me

Village Fancy Dress Party in 1919.   1. Benjamin Bugg, Main Street.   2. Billy Falkner.   3. Arthur Hipwell, Main Street.   4. Mr. Mansbridge, Post Office.   5. Jonathan Oliff, Milton House. 6. Walter Sawford, 7 Ellistown.   7. George Riddle, 1 Ellistown (the village police constable). 8. Frank Knibbs, Grange Farm Cottages.   9. John Haines.   10. Fred Sawbridge, Three Chimneys.   11. Mr. Sawbridge, 6 Ellistown.   12. Mrs. Tier.   13. Mr. Hipwell.   14. H. Hall,

10 Ellistown.   15. Tom Knibbs, Grange Farm Cottages.   16. Richard Knibbs, Grange Farm
Cottages.   17. Arthur Sturgess, 2 Ellistown (the author).   18. G. Johnson, Three Chimneys.
19. Mrs. Whattam.   20. William Davenport.   21. John Rippin, New Inn.   22. Mr. Sawbridge,
6 Ellistown.   23. Joe Loasby, Paradise Row.   24. Percy Ulph, Main Street.   25. George
(Towser) Chapman, 8 Ellistown.   26. Mrs. Sawford.

time to check the trees and learn the different varieties: oak,
ash, spruce, fir, larch, pine.

The Manager gave me a plan of the site, with a planting diagram
showing the distance between the trees and the distance between
the rows. The trees were $10''$–$12''$ high. He explained the procedure: 12 men working in pairs, one with the spade, the other
with an armful of trees. I was to prepare the trees in the right
order for each man.

The day the men were to arrive, we were out bright and early.
We saw a gang of men making towards us and the Manager
exclaimed: 'My God!' As the men got nearer I recognized two of
them: Jack Austin and Gus Wright. Austin was O.K. but Wright
came from a notorious family, in and out of prison most of the
time. There was also a big fellow with a black patch over one eye
and about three days' growth of beard. I should not have been
surprised if one of the twelve had had a wooden leg and a parrot
on his shoulder.

The Manager suddenly remembered a job he had to do further
down the site and as he went away he said: 'I think you had better
take charge. I shall not be here all the time, you know, and it
would be better for you if you gave them their orders from the
start.' This gang looked as if they had just landed from a pirate
ship. Even without the skull and crossbones on their hats they
would have frightened Long John Silver himself.

Patch was leading as he came up to me, he said: 'Who's in
charge?' 'I am.' I said. 'Oh, er . . . I mean, who's the boss?' I
pointed him out to Patch about a quarter of a mile away. 'But
I'm the foreman.'

Patch turned to his mates. 'Look what we have for a foreman,
a bloody kid!' After they had had a good laugh I asked them for
their green cards from the Labour Exchange. I collected all the
cards, then proceeded to give them instructions as to how we
should work: in pairs, one with spade, one with trees, and they
could change over to suit themselves. 'So pair up, and six men,
one from each pair, come with me.'

I handed a spade to each man. The other six I called over to the
stack of trees and explained the planting order. Everything went
well until we got to Patch. I said, 'Come on, take up your trees.'
'I'm not taking orders from a kid.' A long pause. 'Don't be daft,

man.' 'Who are you calling daft?' His attitude was now menacing as he came towards me and I had to think quickly. I felt quite a lot depended on this first encounter. I swallowed hard, and then shouted so all could hear: 'O.K., then, go back to the Labour Exchange and tell them you've got the sack. But don't forget I have your green card and if you do get the sack you will lose six weeks' dole money.'

There was a chorus from the gang: 'Come on, let's get started,' and Patch picked up his trees. So the work was under way and I heaved a big sigh of relief. I knew there was a penalty for refusing work but I didn't know what it was. Neither, apparently, did they.

The work proceeded well after that. Most of them were decent chaps once you got to know them and they were glad of the extra money to see them over Christmas. The job lasted me well into the New Year. Then it was a question of 'What's next?' Sixty years later, by the way, the trees are still going well, some about forty feet high.

Another new digger, No. 4, had been erected in the ironstone pits. Brother George had got the fireman's job and Dad, who had been promoted to foreman fitter, wanted me to take a job with his old friend who was the manager of an engineering works in Kettering. It was that or the farm so I agreed. The wage was 25 shillings per week. I didn't like that after being a foreman at £2.10s.

My new job was quite interesting. I was taught to operate several machines: milling, shaping, capstan lathe etc. I liked the variety and cycling to and from Kettering kept me in good shape for football and cricket. We organised dances now to raise funds for the cricket and football clubs. Life wasn't too bad. Industry however was in a bad way, many men were unemployed, orders were hard to come by as we were suffering from the aftermath of the War. I was not surprised therefore when our firm went on short time and as we only got paid for when we were working my wage was not worth cycling in to Kettering for. I tried to make up with a bit of poaching. There were plenty of rabbits about and after being up half the night I would take my catch into Kettering to sell to the shops at 4d and 6d a time; this helped but I could see I should never be a millionaire at this rate.

After cricket practice one day John Church said he wanted a word with me. He had taken a job as footman in a big house at

Maidwell Hall, as it was in 1919 when Arthur worked there in the stables.

Cottesbrook, and he had heard they wanted a groom at Maidwell Hall and was I interested. Oh yes indeed. He was starting the next day so I agreed to join him. We shared the first part of the journey, then he took the road to Cottesbrook, and I went on to enquire about the job at Maidwell Hall. I had no difficulty in finding the stable yard and as I entered a man asked if he could help. He was about 45 years of age, a bit taller than me. He had rather a long face and spoke with a slight Irish accent. He wore a typical groom's outfit, riding breeches, cloth leggings etc. Yes, they did need a groom, so we had the usual questions and answers interview but at the end of it, it was settled I got the job, starting Monday morning 6.30 a.m. and the wage was £2.5 shillings per week.

It was rather a long journey over rough roads which I couldn't do every day so I had to get lodgings. There was a Loddington family living in the village named Drage so I thought I would start with them. Bill Drage worked on a farm and lived in an adjoining cottage a few minutes from the stables. Mrs. Drage came to the door so I explained who I was and she invited me in. Over a cup of tea I asked if she could cope with a lodger. She told me, if I could put up with four young children, I could have the back bedroom. The price was 15/- per week so I agreed to join them for the evening meal the following Monday.

With my case packed, I started off just before 5 o'clock and arrived at the stables a little before 6.30 a.m. The groom had just finished the first feed. He told me his name was Matchett and as there was no hunting that day he would have a quick breakfast and then we would take the team out for exercise. He brought me a nice hot mug of tea, then we saddled up and were away. For the first half hour his eyes were glued on me, noting my every movements. I pretended not to notice that we both had a lead horse and as time went on he began to relax. After a little more than two hours we were back at the stables without mishap. Then the chores started — mucking out, grooming the horses, carrying in fresh bedding etc. After feeding the horses it was time for our mid-day meal. After the meal there was an hour spent cleaning 'harness'. I was pleased to know Matchett followed the time honoured custom for all grooms, the 'Siesta'. This was the time for our ablutions, wash and shave, cleaning shoes, cup of tea and your feet up for half an hour. I missed Mrs. Johnson's chunk of rice cake.

Then we were off again — feeding, watering, shake down the bedding and making our charges comfortable for the night, so that by 6 o'clock with the work all done, the rest of the day was your own.

The Drage's made me welcome and had a good meal ready for me. We sat up talking for an hour or so then, as I had had rather a busy day I was ready for bed. Bill carried my case up the narrow well worn stairs saying 'It's not much, but I think you will be alright.' He left me to unpack. I didn't expect the Ritz but I got quite a shock as I looked around. The floor boards were completely bare; a small chest of drawers, a single size bed and a chair completed the furnishings. Looking up I thought, well, I shall have no trouble with the ceiling — there wasn't one! The sheets were nice and clean and, laying back, I had a beautiful view of a star-lit sky. Thinking this was no time to study astrology I was soon fast asleep.

At 5.30 a.m., Bill gave me a call, and while he cooked me a good breakfast I had a cold wash in the kitchen sink.

Matchett was busy with the first feed. After his breakfast he told me Reggie* and his wife would both be out hunting that day. Reggie's wife was a titled lady in her own right and must be addressed as 'My Lady'. I took her horse and helped her to mount. She was a very nice lady, and after a little chat she rode away saying that she hoped I would soon settle in. Reggie came up to the stableyard for his horse, mounted, and rode away without a word.

We exercised the other horses and carried on with the usual chores. By evening both horses were back from hunting, and covered with mud. They had been out all day and the mud was set hard on their legs: it took nearly two hours' hard work to get them clean. Next morning I suggested to Matchett we should start clipping: he agreed and said it should have been done before, but he just hadn't had time.

There were four hunters, and a grey cob that Reggie used as a hack around the farm. The hunters were well bred, about four years old. Reggie had two: a big black beauty with not a speck

---

* Reginald Loder, B.A., J.P., of Maidwell Hall.

of white on him except in his eyes — a sign of bad temper. No wonder Matchett always seemed nervous in his box. The other was a nice chestnut and much quieter. Lady Margaret had two mares, one bay and one brown, easy to handle.

Horses do not like to be clipped and they don't like the sound of the machine. This is a contraption on a wooden stand with a handle like an old-fashioned wringer. The clippers are on the end of a 6 ft. cable. The machine that Matchett dragged in was older than anything in the British Museum and very rusty. Matchett said his wife would turn the handle when we were ready.

There were two methods of keeping a horse quiet for this operation: one was to hold up the front leg, the other was the twitch. Matchett preferred the twitch. This is a short pole with a hole drilled through about two inches from the end. A length of sash cord is threaded through and tied to make a loop. The loop goes round the horse's top lip and the pole is then tightened to suit. This needs an experienced man so as not to get the rope too tight.

Mrs. Matchett was called to turn the handle, with Matchett on the twitch and I on the clippers. She was a well-built lady with a loud voice but she didn't bother to use it on me. She always called her husband "Matchett" and he always jumped to obey her commands. We started on one of the quietest mares but she got very upset every time I put the clippers near. Mrs. Matchett started giving orders in a loud voice and this added to the confusion. I suggested we should call it a day and in the meantime I would, with Matchett's permission, have a look at the clippers. She was yapping on about not having all day to waste but I ignored her and walked away.

The Matchetts had a son who was a pale-faced, delicate child; I guessed about six years old. If he ventured into the yard, a sharp command from the kitchen sent him scurrying back. I took the machine into the harness room, dismantled it and cleaned it with paraffin. I oiled it well after I had sharpened it, and the next day we had another go. This time, after Mrs. Matchett had asked sarcastically if we were sure we had got it right, everything went like clockwork, and Matchett had the easiest job of the lot. The next time they came in from hunting the hosepipe soon removed the mud as there was no hair for it to stick to.

The next week we had company. Reggie had engaged a chauffeur who was a nice young chap, but he was from London and village life didn't suit him. He only lasted a week but that was long enough for me to learn a little about motor cars. Reggie had a large four-seater tourer, Lady Margaret a two-seater coupé. The chauffeur taught me how to start it, change gear and turn it around and back and forward in the yard. By the time he was ready to go, I could take each car out of the garage and put it back. I pulled Matchett's leg, telling him I should leave the stables and apply for the chauffeur's job.

One day, Matchett told me he had to do a job in the village with Old Bob in the station waggon. I didn't know Old Bob. Matchett took a rope halter and went to fetch him from the field while I had a look at the station waggon. It was a lightweight affair, with four wheels and metal tyres (the one at Loddington had rubber tyres) two seats up front and an open truck body with slatted sides.

When Matchett returned about half an hour later he was red in the face and out of breath. He had had difficulty in catching the 'Old Divil'. What I saw on the end of that halter was difficult to believe. An old horse with a big head held low, a thin neck, ribs sticking out like fence rails, hips standing up like camel humps and a backbone bent with age — he looked a picture of misery. I said, 'You had difficulty catching this?' Matchett claimed he was a 'Wicked Old Sod'.

He kept turning round and round and I couldn't get his halter on. He was the most pitiful animal I had ever seen so I looked in his mouth where his teeth were black and very loose. No wonder he looked thin with those teeth! He wouldn't be able to gnaw the grass, he was starving on his feet.

I helped to harness him to the waggon and Matchett drove slowly out of the yard. They were back in about an hour, Matchett saying he could have done the job quicker with a wheelbarrow. I expressed my surprise that a man in Reggie's position should own a horse in that condition. I said I would report him to the R.S.P.C.A. and Matchett would be charged with aiding and abetting. Matchett began to tremble at the mention of Reggie's name and begged me not to be so silly. I had noticed Matchett getting very agitated whenever Reggie was about, and now I asked him the reason. 'Ah, you don't know him yet. Wait till you've been here a while — you'll see.'

Things were going along well at my lodgings. The children were put to bed soon after supper and then I would chat with the Drages or read. It was early to bed, early to rise for me. Mrs. Drage had put a mat at the side of my bed; I feared she would spoil me! I knew they must be having a struggle to keep a family of six on about £2 a week. She asked me how I was getting along with Reggie. I told her: 'Very well. But in fact I don't see much of him.' Events showed that I spoke too soon.

The next day, at 'Siesta' time, Matchett nearly had a fit when I offered to take him for a car ride, so I took some dusters and went to play around with the cars. I had finished dusting and was about to leave the garage when Bruton came dashing by, followed by Reggie. He pulled up about a yard from me, glaring and shouting: 'Have you seen Bruton?' 'No.' 'No, what?' 'No, sir.' I was struck dumb, rooted to the spot. He beckoned me to stand aside but I couldn't move. Our eyes met for about a tenth of a second; then he walked round me and went off in the direction Bruton had taken.

I stook there for a few seconds to collect my wits. As I turned to walk back to the harness room I saw Matchett's white face pressed against the window. He opened the door and showered me with questions. 'What did he say?' 'What did he want?' 'What did you say?' I didn't answer because a gleam of an idea had started to form in my mind but I wanted more time to think it out. Then I said, 'That was quite an experience. There's no chance of a cup of tea, I suppose?'

He was off like a shot. During the incident I had had my back to Matchett so he couldn't see whether I had spoken or not. He was back in a few minutes. Banging two mugs of tea on the table, he said, 'Now tell me what he said. What went on out there? Come on, tell me.' I could see he was beside himself, hopping from one foot to the other. I took a drink of tea. Long pause. 'I put him in his place.' 'What! You did what? Oh, my God.' Matchett dropped into his chair. 'That's done it, that's done it! We shall all get the bloody sack now. Oh, my God, what have you done?'

I told him I would teach him to drive a car and we would both get jobs as chauffeurs. He spent the rest of the afternoon asking questions and calling me all the unflattering names he could think of. That night I lay thinking about the day's events. I had caught a quick glimpse into Reggie's eyes and what I had seen wasn't madness, nor anger, nor fear. I concluded I had seen nothing I need be afraid of . . .

I was suddenly awakened by a big blob of cold water on my cheek. I lit the candle, pushed the bed up against the wall, and went in search of a bucket. I found one in the kitchen and placed it to catch the drips. Then I went off to sleep to the sound of 'Plop, plop, plop' in the bucket.

I couldn't get Old Bob out of my mind. I plied Matchett with questions but all he would say was: 'Old Bob has always been around, he was here when I came.' I thought of the old horse dying on his feet and decided to pay him a visit. I took a bowl of Reggie's best crushed oats and found Bob standing all alone in the shelter of a tall hedge. He dug in hungrily; though his front teeth were loose he could chew all right with the back ones. It took some time to clear the bowl, so the next day I found an old wooden bucket, fixed it firmly in the hedge roots, and emptied the oats in. After that, I would run down to the paddock every day with his feed.

Hunting was now in full swing, Reggie would occasionally require a second horse and that meant Matchett would have to meet him with a fresh horse and bring the tired one home. This was all extra work but it was all part of the job.

One day Matchett had to go to Lamport Station for a parcel and as he had to take the bay mare for exercise he said he would call for the parcel on his way back. I finished my chores and decided to pop down to the village Post Office on my bike. The reader will probably know that all stable doors are in two halves, the idea being to open the top half during the daytime to let in the fresh air. When I got back from the Post Office the bottom half of the door was ajar. I assumed Matchett was back so I rode up and rested my arm on the lower door and, looking over, I saw the bridle and saddle had been taken off and Matchett was in the act of lifting a rather heavy wooden bucket full of water for the mare to drink. His face was red with the effort and the mare was just about to drink, when, in a loud whisper I said 'How's Reggie?' What happened next was totally unexpected. The bucket dropped with a crash. The startled mare swerved quickly knocking Matchett into the water running down the stable floor. I put my bike up quickly then, looking over the door, I was in time to see him getting up. I said 'You will be in trouble if your wife sees you rolling about in that water.' The language that followed couldn't be printed and although I protested my innocence, he vowed he would 'Swing for me yet.'

Matchett was not a man to 'sulk' for long, after a cigarette he soon began to relax and we enjoyed a good laugh. The day after the incident with Reggie, Mrs. Matchett appeared at the harness room door with a tray, two cups of tea, sugar and milk. She had a bit of lipstick on and a clean pinafore. She smiled at me and asked 'How many sugar? Shall I pour?' I was almost speechless but managed to stutter 'Two please'. She tried hard to make conversation. I don't know what her husband had told her, but I was convinced he had given her a colourful and exaggerated account of my encounter with Reggie. She never missed a day after that and continued her efforts to be friendly.

Horses like carrots and it was my task to see that a good supply was always available. They were delivered by the cartload from the farm. I had to wash them and for this I had a round wooden tub and could wash about a week's supply at a time. I told Matchett there was no bath at my lodgings and asked permission to use the tub. He readily agreed and produced two large saucepans. These I filled with soft water, then made up the fire. By the time I had scrubbed the tub out and put in the cold, the hot water was ready and with a half pound of Lifebouy soap I was able to enjoy a good bath. I could only manage one once a week but that was better than nothing.

Most weekends I managed to get home for a few hours. It depended on the weather. I would have an evening with the Gang — stay the night at home and cycle back the next morning. Christmas was no different. The animals had to be fed, but I managed to get home for Christmas dinner because Matchett offered to do the evening feed on his own.

Severe frost came in with the New Year and hunting was abandoned for a time. This meant more work for us; we had to exercise the horses in the fields one at a time. They thought they were out hunting. It was difficult to hold them until they had done a good gallop. The soft ground by the brook along the

Draughton Dales was ideal for this purpose. Matchett would go down to the Hall every morning to get the orders for the day and these would be passed on to him by the cook.

One morning he came back looking a bit down in the mouth. We had to take Old Bob to do a little job in the village. Four empty crates were to be collected from a farm and delivered to the Hall. He grumbled about having to catch that old 'Divil', so I offered to fetch him. 'Watch him,' he said, 'he's crafty. Take this halter but don't let him see it.' Saying I didn't need a halter, I ran off down the drive. I knew Bob fairly well. I should do as I fed him every day. When I opened the gate Bob looked up as usual. I suppose he thought, 'Ah, crushed oats' and when he came shuffling along I turned and went back up the drive. I didn't know whether he would follow or not – but he did – and within five minutes we were back at the yard. 'Hells, bells', said Matchett, 'How on earth did you do that?' 'I just had a word in his ear,' I said. We soon had him harnessed to the station waggon and taking up the reins Matchett announced 'I will drive.'

I climbed into the passenger seat and away we went. I don't know whether Bob was in a bad mood or disappointed at not getting his oats, but he was definitely operating the 'Go Slow'. Matchett shook the reins and gave him a few strikes with the whip but it made no difference; one step, then another, that was all he was prepared to do. 'It will be dark before we get there,'' said Matchett, 'have a word with him.' 'Not I,' I said, 'you're the driver.'

At last we arrived and it didn't take long to load up. Matchett said, 'Will you drive back then?' Unknown to him, I had been running my hands over Bob when I took his daily feed and I had discovered his weakness – a ticklish back. When I ran my hand down his back-bone he would get quite excited and lash out with his back feet. I didn't know if it would work but it was worth a try. I had a plan in mind while Matchett sat back with a cynical grin as if to say 'Now lets see what you can do, Mr. Clever Dick.' I addressed myself to Bob. 'Come on, Bob, I want you to show Mr. Matchett what you can do. Gee up then.' Bob started to move very slowly. Turning to Matchett I said, 'Watch his ears, keep your eyes fixed on his ears.' Then make great play with the reins, I leaned forward and pushed the whipstock sharply along his back-bone. I was quite unprepared for what happened next. Giving a little 'neigh' his head came up with a jerk, his tail stood up like a brush, his front feet pawed the air, and then we were away. Making a half turn we shot out on to the road, then down the village street as if the 'Seven devils of Sligo' were after us. Sparks and pebbles flew from the wheels as we turned off the road and on through the main gates, missing the near post by about half an inch. Matchett was laying back gripping the seat with both hands as we dashed down the drive. An overhanging laurel branch whipped off his cap and with a sharp right turn we pulled up at the back door in a flurry of gravel and dust. I jumped down and ran to the horse's head. Hatless, Matchett jumped down and ran to the lavatory. The outward journey had taken about half an hour — the return journey about three minutes. It took several minutes of soothing and patting before Bob settled down. I unloaded the crates just as Matchett came through the back door. His face was whiter and longer; his lips drooped at the ends and with his hair all ruffled he looked a picture of misery. I asked him what he was laughing at, but all he said was 'Jesus, what a ride.' I offered to take him back to the yard, but he replied in a weak voice 'I've lost my cap.'

As an extra treat, I sliced some carrots and mixed them with the crushed oats. When I left him Bob was munching away and seemed to be fully recovered. Back in the harness room Matchett was still very quiet, but he livened up when his wife, complete with her lipstick, pinafore and tray of tea entered. The tea having revived his spirits, he gave his wife a colourful account of our latest escapade — laughter came easy that day.

It was then back to work. When I told Matchett the next day about Bob's daily feed he nearly had a fit, saying 'If Reggie gets to know you have been feeding his best oats to that bundle of bones he will shoot you on the spot.'

With Spring well on the way we realised the hunting season would soon be over. Lady Margaret was going to London for an extended holiday and would not be hunting again. Reggie however continued as usual his three days a week. The cars were not used much but when they did go out it was extra work for me washing and cleaning. I didn't mind this for in fact I enjoyed driving them in and out of the garage. And so life went on but we little knew then how soon it would change.

I went home as usual on the Sunday evening after a night out with the boys. I was up and made an early start to Maidwell. As I entered the stable yard I noticed the stable lights were not on. Matchett should have been giving the first feed. There was a small light in his kitchen window and after waiting about ten minutes I was about to go and call him, when Mrs. Matchett came out, obviously very distressed. She told me he had taken his usual Sunday evening walk over to Lamport Pub to see a friend when a man on a cycle had run into him and he was in Northampton Hospital with critical head injuries. I assured her I would look after the horses and if I could help in any way she was to call me. Mid morning a message came through to say Matchett was dead.

Reggie hunted as usual. He was late coming in and by the time I had put his horse up for the night I was 'all in' but I couldn't sleep. I suppose it was shock from the day's events. Next day I was summoned to appear before the 'Great Man himself'. I had a word with the cook and she showed me to Reggie's door. I supposed he wanted to talk to me about Matchett and the running of the stables. I didn't like the man, but he was paying my wages and I must show respect to a man in his station. Taking off my cap I knocked on the door. He shouted 'Come in.' It was a large room with windows overlooking the lawns and lake beyond. He sat at his desk at the far end of the room. I was about to walk towards his desk when he shouted 'Get back on that mat.' I jumped back as if I had been shot. Without any preliminary and no mention of Matchett, he told me he would only be hunting for a short while and as Lady Margaret was away he assumed I could manage. All orders in future would be passed to me through the cook — that was all.

It had suddenly occurred to me to try the 'Oliver Twist'. I hadn't opened my mouth so far and now I asked for permission to speak. I enquired, 'As there would be quite a lot of extra work, had he given any thought to extra pay?' He replied, 'No, but you can have an extra 5/-' — end of interview.

After the inquest Matchett was laid to rest and Reggie lost no time in giving Mrs. Matchett notice to quit the house. As a temporary measure she was given a small cottage in the village. With Matchett gone and the house empty one could cut the silence. I wanted to leave at once but the thought of the horses kept me there. Exercising them and the general care of the team made it a long day. I trotted down to see the cook every morning. One day she told me the papers had not been delivered and as they were at Lamport Station would I collect them. I decided to take the black horse as he needed more exercise than the others. It had started to rain, — just a few spots but I thought I should be back in a few minutes so I didn't bother to take a mac. I collected the papers and started back when the rain came faster. I thought I would push on, urging my mount to do still more but I forgot Townsend's advice. The horse's head went down and I landed in a gateway of thick black mud. I managed to hold on to the reins and retrieving the papers from the mud. The cook managed to clean them and I heard no more.

It was all go now and I would exercise my team two at a time. I was out one day walking the horses towards Draughton Crossing when a man and two terriers suddenly jumped through a gap in the hedge. One horse went one way, one the other and I on my back in the middle of the road. I jumped up to tell the man what I thought of him when I recognised Frank Johnson; but my horses came before him. Fortunately the crossing gates were closed and I soon mounted one and caught the other. I felt that if I had fought Johnson that day I could have beaten him.

I continued to give old Bob his feed and although he looked a lot better he was a very old horse and I feared he was on his last legs. Reggie announced through the cook that he was finished hunting for the Season and would soon be going to Africa, big game hunting. She told me the four crates we had collected from the farm were now filled with the best silver from the Hall and I was to harness old Bob into the station waggon and take the silver to the Bank in Northampton. I protested the old horse would never make it for he might die on the way, but she said 'Orders is orders.'

Playing for time, I told cook it would take two days to prepare for the journey. She assumed that would be alright, so I spent the time with Bob giving him three meals a day of crushed oats and sliced carrots. I groomed him, trimmed his mane and tail, and examined his feet. This was new treatment for him and he loved it.

Bruton helped me to load up the crates and with a letter for the

Bank Manager we were on our way by 9 o'clock. Mrs. Drage cut me some sandwiches and with an extra meal for Bob we made for the open road. I just let him go at his own pace and because I had fed my team before I left I had all day if necessary. It must have been about 12.30 when we arrived at Northampton — the factory workers were just knocking off for dinner. It didn't take long to find the Bank so, handing my letter to a clerk who soon returned with two helpers, they unloaded my waggon. I managed to get a bucket of water for Bob then fixed his nose-bag. I left him with his favourite meal while I went in to the Bank to wait for my receipt. I didn't have to wait long for the Manager came out and thanked me and I sat in my waggon and ate my sandwiches.

As I expected the journey back was slow and tedious. It was only the fact that we were heading for home that kept Bob going. We passed through Brixworth, then on to Lamport, over the Crossing and now for Hopping Hill. I stopped for half an hour to give him a rest before climbing the hill. I got out and pushed up the steepest part, but it was touch and go. I took hold of his bridle and walked the rest of the way but by the time we reached the stable yard his head was almost on the ground. It had taken us over 4 hours to do the 12 miles. He followed me down to the field and watched me put a feed of oats in the bucket but he made no move towards it. I left him standing there as I still had my team to feed. Next day he was much brighter but his legs were very stiff and it took him several days to recover.

Now that hunting was finished the horses had to be roughed-off before they were turned out to grass. The rugs were taken off; there was no more grooming and by tradition they should go out on May 1st.

I called on the cook as usual and she told me Reggie was leaving the next day. I was to take him and all his luggage to Lamport Station using old Bob and the station waggon. I arrived in plenty of time. Cook helped with the luggage and Reggie took his seat by my side. It took a long time to get to the Station but Reggie made no complaint. He took up a position at the end of the platform while the porter helped me with the luggage. When the trained pulled in he waited to see all his gear stowed away then, turning to me, he handed me an envelope and then took his seat in the carriage without a word.

I opened the envelope and found two weeks wages and a long list of instructions — some of the instructions I didn't like.

'Turn out all the horses immediately.'

'Wash cars and cover with dust sheets.'

'Clean out all stables. Wash walls and floors. Disinfect all drains etc.'

'Take the old pony to Brixworth Kennels for dog meat.'

I took the list to the cook. When she read it through she said 'Well, that's it, you have your orders.' I told her I was willing to do all the other jobs but I would not take old Bob to the Kennels. But she was adamant, saying there is no one else and 'Orders is orders.'

In my opinion it was too cold to turn the horses out so I delayed this as long as I could. After a week however I had to let them out to get on with cleaning the stables. I didn't do anything about Bob hoping something would turn up. All my cleaning was done except the harness room, but I couldn't settle to this and taking a rope halter saying, 'It has only got to be done once', I collected Bob from the field. I had to take my bike in order to get back. Bob didn't like me riding the bike and he seemed to sense there was something wrong. He wouldn't co-operate and it was a difficult journey.

I had been told there was a 10/- tip for anyone taking a horse for dog meat. When I asked the groom at the kennels about this he said, 'Oh, that's been discontinued', so I told him 'In that case I shall take my horse back', 'Hold on,' he said, 'I'll go and enquire.' He was back in a few minutes with a 10/- note. I took Bob into the stable where the groom placed a bell-like appliance on his forehead and bang — Bob was no more.

The next day I set out spring cleaning the harness room. I cleaned and polished the grate, scrubbed the table top and was just finishing the floor when I had a visitor. He told me he was Reggie's brother and had come at his brother's request to make a final inspection before I left. After his tour he gave me a £5 note expressed his complete satisfaction and told me I was free to leave at my own convenience. I handed the keys to the cook and I was away.

Mrs. Drage shed a few tears as I packed my case. I gave her an extra week's board in lieu of notice and then called on Mrs.

Matchett. There were more tears as we said goodbye. She looked a pitiful figure standing in the doorway with her pale-faced son standing by her side. Laughter was hard to come by, and Reggie was still an enigma.

Back home I was told brother George was leaving to drive the No. 4 Digger. Dad had got me a job in the mines as a 'Steam Pump Driver'. At $15\frac{1}{2}$ I was under age but the Manager thought it would be alright if we all kept quiet about it. My job was to pump water from the stream to two reservoirs where the water was then fed to the digger by 'Gravity'. The stream was dammed and the pump was situated at a very quiet spot. I often worked all day without seeing a soul. This was very boring but I was told I was lucky to have a job as there was over two million unemployed. After about six months the Company decided to move No. 4 Digger across the fields to open up a new pit at Orton. I was promoted to be the Fireman for brother George and after a week training we started a double shift system 6–2 and 2–10.

For the early shift I had to be up at 4 a.m. to get steam up and all ready for a 6 o'clock start. George bought a motor bike; a smart looking machine. It was a $2\frac{1}{4}$ h.p. 'Silver Prince' – a two stroke engine with a Villiers flywheel magneto. This machine, I was assured, was capable to doing up to 35 m.p.h. These figures impressed me so much I was a 'motor bike man' from now on, delving into the mysteries of the 'internal combustion engine'.

I had saved a few pounds and when George decided to have a bigger machine I became the owner of the 'Silver Prince'. I had a cap with a peak at the back and with my goggles set at a determined angle I toured the country lanes at breathtaking speed; much to the consternation of the local folk who considered anything above 10 m.p.h. was fast. When I wasn't riding I was taking it to pieces. Life was passing pleasant.

During May 1921 there were very strong rumours about the mines having to close owing to the lack of orders. Then we got the news that our Auntie had died in Liverpool. Uncle Jack (mother's brother) was coming to spend a weeks holiday with us. We knew very little about our relations but now we learned that mother had this brother in Liverpool and a sister in Birkenhead.

When I learned that Uncle Jack was a builder I looked forward to his visit with anticipation. He brought with him our cousin Fred who was about two years younger than me. After a couple of days I asked him if he could give me a job on the buildings. The subject was discussed several times during his stay and then, after further discussion with my parents, it was agreed I should give it a try, but I was to come home without question if I was not up to the required standard. Uncle Jack went back after a week, leaving Fred with us. I worked a week's notice and followed on with Fred the second week. Dad had taken out a Driving Licence so I left the motor bike with him.

Uncle Jack assured us that as he had plenty of room there would be no need for me to get lodgings and I could stay with them. He would pay my board and give me 10/- per week for the start as pocket money, so I agreed to this as I was not a big spender. It had all been done so quickly I hadn't had much time to think. However I packed my case again and after saying all the goodbyes it was Liverpool here we come . . .

CHAPTER III
Liverpool

Cousin Fred and I walked out of Central Station into the busy Liverpool street. We boarded a tram going to the pier head. This was my first ride on a tram and although I had not even seen one before I was not favourably impressed. We moved forward in jerks while the driver was continually working a lever with one hand and banging the bell with the other. We were in a long stream of trams going one way and there was another stream going the opposite way — it was like Bedlam. There was a network of wires criss-crossing above our heads and a flat copper strip attached to a long pole was making contact with the wires and giving off a series of flashes. I thought 'It's a wonder this place hasn't caught fire before now.'

Most of the other traffic was horse-drawn — tradesmen's delivery vans and carts with big shires pulling the railway drays. I caught sight of a pair of 'Giant Grey's' pulling a brewers dray. There was very little motor traffic about. People were hurrying in all directions. When I was a boy I used to take the top off an ant's nest to watch them at work putting their house back in order. This place was like the ant's nest but the ants moved about in better order.

Swinging around in front of the 'Liver Buildings' our tram stopped with a big shudder at the pier entrance. My eyes must have been as big as saucers as I took in the scene. I think at the back of my mind I had pictured the river as a stream with the ferry boats in the charge of an 'Old Salt', complete with peak cap, shouting '2 pence per person per trip.'

What I did see was to me a vast expanse of water for I had never seen the sea before. It was at least two miles wide at this point and the ferry boats were large fat ships capable of carrying 2,000 people at a time. They heaved up and down on the waves, it taking a little over ten minutes to cross. I gripped the hand rail until my knuckles were white. We landed safely at Seacombe. Fred took me through a series of back streets then suddenly said, 'Here we are'; it was 52 Bisley Street.

The household consisted of Uncle Jack, Lizzie, (his eldest daughter) Bill Ryan her husband, Elsie, about a year younger than me, Fred and myself. There was another cousin Edith married to Will Ferrie but they lived in the next street.

Three bedrooms, front room, living room and kitchen with the lavatory out in the yard and no bathroom. I shared the front bedroom with Uncle Jack and Fred. After two days sightseeing with Fred I started work. Shock No. 2 came when I learned that Uncle Jack was not the builder. He was in partnership with another man named Bob Jones on a brickwork-only contract. However I got stuck in although it was a little confusing at first, but I took to the work like a duck to water. First, the knack of using the trowel, keeping the correct bond for the bricks and plumbing the corners etc. There were few complaints from Uncle Jack so I settled down to give value for money. We moved around the district doing the brickwork for different builders. We did quite a lot of work for a builder named J. Henshaw. His son Jack came to work with us on the buildings and we became good friends. Fred introduced me to the local boys and I was soon a member of 'The Gang'.

There were four football teams within a 2d tram ride. Liverpool and Everton were First Division, Tranmere and New Brighton Third Division.

The Cinema had come in with a bang and new ones were opening up and doing good trade. Theatres were also plentiful. At Tower Theatre, New Brighton, Gracie Fields had just finished a week before going on her first tour to America. At the Empire, Liverpool and the Argyll, Birkenhead, there was also plenty to spend your money on. I liked the Variety at the Argyll best. Later when radio came in there was a regular broadcast every Saturday night. Danny Black was the popular manager and it was a 'Full House' every night so one had to book well in advance. Charlie Chaplin did his last show at the Argyll in the 'Mumming Birds' before he too went to the States. Harry Lauder was another big star Danny Black had on his books. Birkenhead was not the safest place to be late on a Saturday night. We never went with less than four in our Gang. We walked across the 'Four Bridges', over the Docks and past the Dock Board tenements. The police always patrolled in threes carrying long white truncheons and they rattled the pavement with them when they needed assistance.

The people in our locality were very friendly. Every weekend there would be a 'do' on at one or other house; a few drinks, a sing song around the piano, and always a game of cards in the back room. You just threw your cap in and if it didn't come straight out you were welcome.

Nearly everyone had a bet on the horses. The baker's rounds-man would collect the betting slips when he delivered the bread. I was very keen on football at home and when I made enquiries I was told I could get a game at the back of the Sandy Belt works. I discovered this was a large area of waste land with ashes in place of grass where several Gangs were kicking a ball about but it wasn't my idea of football so I took no part. I explored the area while I was there and was suprised to find gambling in all its forms in full swing. A large crowd was watching the 'whippit racing'. One man would hold the dog while the owner, carrying a coloured cloth, would walk down the course to the winning post. Usually there were six dogs in each race and at the drop of the flag each dog raced to its owner who would be waiting and waving his own particular colour cloth. Most of these men were unemployed but the bookies were doing good business with plenty of £1 notes in evidence.

One Gang was playing 'Housie Housie' (Bingo), another was on Pitch and Toss and several card schools were in progress. All this was illegal but there were no police in sight.

The far side was allotment fields and here I found every plot holder had a pigeon loft. These birds were bred especially for racing and their owners were standing around in small groups waiting for the first birds home having betted on the results.

I used to like a game of cards — Solo, Whist etc. When the Gang asked me if I would like a game I readily agreed but they were too fast and slick for me so I lost heavily.

After a bout of 'home sickness' I wrote a letter home to let them know I was alright. I tried my hand at cards several times during the following week but the result was always the same so I crossed cards off my list of activities. The 10/- per week I was getting from Uncle Jack didn't go far and my reserve of capital dwindled alarmingly. After eight months I felt I was making good progress with my bricklaying and asked him for a rise, but I must have chosen the wrong time — no luck — and was advised to try again later. About two weeks after that however, Uncle Jack came to me with a proposition. A builder, Mr. Forshaw, wanted the brickwork done for two pairs of houses at Heswell, out in the country. If I wanted to win my spurs, as he put it, here was my chance. Get them up by Christmas and my request for extra pay would be considered. I accepted the challenge, for after all I had nothing to lose.

Cousin Fred had joined the firm by now and was becoming quite useful with the trowel. He came with me. We had a good labourer and as the weather was fine we made a good start. We completed the first pair and, racing against time, we were well on with the second when I caught a severe cold. A bad cough developed and although I tried every cough cure I could find, it just got worse. I very much wanted to complete the job. The second pair were now three-quarters built but I was feeling quite ill. After coughing up some blood I went to see the doctor who was about thirty-five and Irish. While I got dressed he mixed some medicine then told me I had pleurisy. Taking my arm he said, "Come on, I'll take you home.' Before he left he saw me into bed and then, after painting my side with iodine, gave Lizzie instructions about the medicine and promised to call again next day. I shall always be grateful to that young doctor, he saved my life.

I had promised to go home for Christmas, but I didn't think I should be able to travel so I wrote home giving them the full details. Two days later Mother and Dad arrived, and after a short stay they took me back home. Under Mother's expert nursing I soon recovered and in two weeks I was ready to return. I made a full report of my progress and I was anxious to get back to my work. Mother understood all this but insisted I stay another week to make sure I was fully recovered. Uncle Jack explained he had to get another bricklayer to finish the second pair of houses and as he had nothing for me, I was to go back to his partner, Bob Jones. I knew Bob but I had never worked with him. I found him to be a man of few words. He explained that while I was working for him, he would be paying my wages and I should have to pay my own board. At the end of the week I was pleased when he paid me £2. Lizzie however required £1.10s. board, so I was no better off!

Fred came in one day to say a man a few doors away had a motor bike but he couldn't start it, would I help? I explained I wasn't a mechanic, but I would have a look. I found the timing had slipped; a common fault. I reset the timing and to the surprise of everyone including myself, it started first kick. I didn't want payment for my services but he insisted on me taking a packet of cigarettes. I was able to help him on several occasions after that and we became friends. He told me his name was Tom Jones. He was a general foreman for a big firm of contractors and if I needed a job at anytime just let him know.

Advertised in the local paper I spotted — Motor Cycle for sale, needs attention, cheap. After a good hour bargaining I bought it for £1.5s. I put it in order and cleaned it. Fred found a buyer at £2.10s. After that I was soon doing good business, buying and selling old motor bikes. I bought all my spare parts from 'Bostocks Cycle and Motorcycle Shop' in Pulton Road. I soon became friendly with Mr. Bostock, a pleasant man about forty. When he knew what I was doing he gave me a lot of good advice about repairs, and offered me the use of his workshop.

However I was not satisfied with my progress on the buildings. After a year I had only ten shillings per week to spend. Lucky for me my sister Alice had made me two suits and an overcoat before I left home, as I had no money for clothing. Bob Jones was not prepared to pay any extra so there was only one thing to do; look for another job!

Albert Walters (my labourer), was also dissatisfied with his job. He told me he could get work on the new site where the Corporation were building a new estate on the waste land at the back of Sandy Belt works. They were trying a new idea which was steel framework with a brick outer skin. There would be inside work for the winter and he was keen to get in at the start. He could have a job if he took a bricklayer and would I go with him? I would. The new site was only a few minutes away. At five o'clock 'knocking off' time, we ran like rabbits to catch the foreman before he left. Walters said, 'Don't forget to tell him you are a Journeyman.' That means you have finished your apprenticeship. The foreman was locking his office door when I asked 'Do you need bricklayers?' He took a long look at me. 'How old are You?' 'Twenty.' 'You don't look it. Are you a journeyman?'

'Yes.' Quite a lot of questions later he asked who was I working for now. When I told him he said 'Jack Jones? I know him well enough. He uses the same pub as me. O.K. start when you have worked your notice.' Bob Jones didn't seem surprised when I told him. Just said I could leave at the end of the week.

With Walters as my labourer we started on the Monday morning. We were about the first on the site. The Foreman worked with us on the foundations for a while, then as other bricklayers started we soon had a team going. For 44 hours a week at 1/6d an hour, my wages were now £3.6s. per week. I'm moving up!

This was a good job for me. I learned many tricks of the trade and 'upmanship' was well to the fore.

The size of the workforce increased rapidly as new tradesmen joined us. Carpenters, plumbers, plasterers, etc. A new mate came to join me. His name was Hugh Hardman, about 35, taller than me, slim build, trilby hat and pince-nez. With his pale complexion he didn't look the part, but he was a pleasant chap and he could lay bricks. I noticed that he had a newspaper out at every opportunity, and soon discovered he was a horse-racing fanatic. What that man didn't know about horse-racing wasn't worth knowing. Owners, trainers, horses for courses, weight and distance — the lot. He had a persuasive tongue and I was soon having a shilling on my fancy. The building site was only two minutes away so I left my bets with Lizzy when I went in for dinner. I wasn't having much luck until one day I had two winners, both at good prices. My calculations told me I had won a little over £3.10s. Alas, when I got in, Lizzy was crying and told me she had forgotten to 'put the bet on'; like the cards I could not win.

Hardman had an account with his bookie and would phone his bets from a box at the end of the street. Soon he was taking bets for other chaps which he didn't mind as he earned a good commission. He would call in at the bookies each evening and bring back the winnings, if any, next day. It soon became obvious to us the bookie was getting the best of the deal. Hardman had what he thought was a brilliant idea. We should 'milk' the bets. He would withhold what he considered to be the losing bets while the likely winners would be phoned to the bookie. We were to be partners in this conspiracy. The scheme went very well indeed and a check up revealed we had £126 in the 'Kitty', until one morning, he came to work with a long face. He had had a wild fling in the bookies office on the Saturday afternoon and lost our 'Kitty'. I was £63 out of pocket. He was full of apologies, of course and promised to pay something off the debt each week. I consoled myself with the thought that I hadn't really lost anything as I had not laid anything out. However from then on, (like the card playing) I crossed horse-racing off my list.

It was about this time a new brickie joined our gang. His name was Arthur Henderson; just the same age as me, with dark hair and a bit taller, (they all were). He was very interested in motor bikes. We soon became friends and he joined the motor bike gang in the back yard. Jack Henshaw was another frequent caller. We had quite a lot in common, and spent most of our time together. Sunday afternoon was different; we often walked along the promenade from Seacombe to New Brighton and watched the big ships of the 'White Star Line' anchor in the river ready for docking on the Monday morning. We would obtain tickets from the shipping office and spend the afternoon exploring the big liners. The Italian fleet once paid a courtesy visit; painted light grey they looked very impressive, cruisers, destroyers, submarines, etc. We spent a very interesting afternoon on these.

Arthur, like myself, was eager to learn all about the building industry. When he told me about the evening classes about to start at the Technical School, I agreed to join. I'm afraid I was at a great disadvantage at first and wished I had paid more attention at school. However, once a week at the 'Tech' and with Arthur's help in between, I emerged at the end of term with reasonable marks. The second term was better and I was glad I had taken the opportunity to learn something about the technical side; Architecture, Scale and Freehand Drawing, Plans and Specifications, etc.

We were still busy on the steel housing site. One wet day the foreman delayed blowing his whistle for us to knock off and take shelter. We were very wet by the time we were able to run to an empty house and light a fire to dry our coats. We had just got a good fire going when a gang of about ten or twelve chaps joined us. They seemed friendly enough, and by their chatter we gathered they were Welsh. After about ten minutes a pleasant tenor voice started to sing, then, one after another, they all came in on cue.

They sang because they enjoyed singing and standing there holding their steaming wet jackets before the fire, they enjoyed themselves to the full. No music, no conductor, they went from song to song, from hymn to hymn. The sound of these human voices blended together in perfect harmony had a profound effect on me. We were told they belonged to a choral society in Birkenhead. I kept a sharp lookout for them and never missed an opportunity to listen to their singing.

Sometimes I rode my motorbike back to work after dinner. With my cap and goggles I would ride around the site — quite the 'Show Off' — but there was a method in my madness. I got quite a few sales like this. Mr. Bostock also got some benefit with quite a lot of enquiries and a few sales of new and secondhand machines. Jack Henshaw's father bought him a new 4 valve Rudge. Mr. Bostock promised he would see me alright for a good bike, by way of commission. My next purchase however was a nearly new 'Rudge Multi' motorbike and sidecar. I was never without a passenger for the sidecar. In turn I took all the members of the family out into the country or to Chester for a row on the river Dee with tea in a little cafe overlooking the river, or to sit in the shade listening to the band. There were only two snags. I had to disconnect the sidecar after every journey to get it up the entry and the other was the gear system. It worked on an expanding pulley on the back wheel and being a belt drive it slipped when it got wet. This was very frustrating. I would sit there in the rain with the engine roaring away but unable to move. Choosing a fine spell I managed to sell it without loss.

Mr. Bostock had taken in a new type overhead valve 4 stroke B.S.A. It seems the customer had failed to keep up the H.P. and I was able to buy this at a very reasonable price. Now, at last, I had a top class machine and with Arthur on the pillion seat and Jack Henshaw on his Rudge, we were able to tour North Wales from Chester to Holyhead.

In the meantime work on the housing site was drawing to a close and it would soon be time to look out for the next job. Work was very hard to come by, so, when I had a letter from home, and they told me amongst other news items, that a new squire was moving into Loddington Hall and having quite a lot of extensions and alterations done. I made up my mind quickly and in no time

I packed a case and with my new bike I was on my way home; this time by road.

The journey was uneventful. The family were pleased to see me and I lost no time in contacting the foreman in charge at the Hall. Yes, he could give me a job and explained that most of the work would be in stone. I was pleased about that as I had not done any stonework. He worked with me the first week, then, with a labourer I was on my own. I found it pleasant and interesting work, better than cottage slogging. I was working at the Hall for several months. The firm then sent me to Kettering to help finish a factory they were building for the Co-operative Clothing Society. My labourer on this job was an old school mate, Harold Bambridge. I used to take him to and from work on my pillion seat. One Bank Holiday, I think it was August, I asked if he would like to go out for the day on the bike. He told me he had an Aunt at Norwich, so off to Norwich we went. We found the Uncle and Aunt after some difficulty. We were made very welcome and told we could stay as long as we liked. The next day after showing us around the town, we climbed up a hill to the 'Mousehole'. This was a plateau used by the local Flying Club.

We talked to the Secretary of the Club who told us we could have a flight for five shillings a time. The plane was a Gipsy Moth which was a small two seater with an open cockpit. By a toss of a coin I was to go first. The pilot, a pleasant faced chap said, 'Hop in, but leave your cap for identification.' This encouraged me a lot so up and away we went. After a few minutes I tried to look down, but the side of the cockpit was too high, so taking a grip of my seat, I heaved myself up to get a better look. At the same time the pilot who was in the seat behind, tilted the plane. I shot back into my seat as if I had been poleaxed. I thought I had been responsible for the plane tilting. I looked back at the pilot who had tears streaming down his cheeks. I had not seen a man laugh like that since I asked Farmer Hargraves for a extra twopence an hour. I think the pilot enjoyed the trip so much he gave me a good five shillings worth. We flew over Yarmouth, a little way out to sea and back over the River Yare. I quite enjoyed it after the first shock.

When the pilot had finished laughing he took my mate up and this experience was a talking point for a long time.

My younger sister, Ruth, had joined Alice at the Clothing Factory. Tom would soon be making plans for when he left school. Doll the youngest and born at Loddington, was now a schoolgirl and making good progress. Dad was riding the 'Silver Prince' to work. George was not satisfied with his work however and questioned me about the prospects of a job in Liverpool.

I was anxious to be back in time for the Autumn Term at the Technical college, so once more I made for the open road and Liverpool. Builder Henshaw was about to start some more houses doing the brickwork with his own men. This just suited me and I had work near home for most of the winter. Early spring however I was again looking for a job. I remembered the offer from Tom Jones and went to see him. He told me his firm had no vacancies at that time but he knew the foreman on another firm who were starting a new school at Morton, on the outer suburb of the town, and to mention his name. After the usual questions and answers the foreman explained that this was first class work and must be done right first time, – quality before quantity, etc., and on Tom Jones' recommendation he would give me a trial starting next day. The first two days I was on foundations with the foreman hovering around, but this time it was 'take your time' not 'get a move on'. This looked like being a big job, but there was only one other bricklayer. The first time I saw him I could hardly believe my eyes. A man about 50, short legs, a good round stomach, and shoulders that tapered to his head, but no neck, and a cap on his head that tapered almost to a point. He looked like a walking 'Cider flagon', this was Ted. The foreman told me I was to work with Ted, and warned me, 'Don't speak to him first, let him start the conversation. It may take a day or two. Don't borrow any of his tools, hammer, foot rule, plumb bob, etc. etc. He is a first class tradesman and you can learn a lot from him.' So I joined Ted. I carried out my instructions to the letter. The third day he said 'Good morning.' Fourth day, 'Good morning, do you want a drink?' He offered me a pint bottle of Brown Ale. 'No thanks, I don't drink.' The fifth day he sat beside me to have his lunch and then he got going. He had two pint bottles of ale for his lunch, two for his dinner, two for his supper. The foreman's advice paid off and gradually we became friends. 'Two pint Ted' I called him. During the months that followed he proved to be not only a good tradesman, but also a good teacher, cutting and turning arches, bonding brickwork to stone, cutting and setting stone heads, cills and mullions, glaze brickwork on interior walls. etc. Other brick-layers were set on and we soon had a full team, but Ted and I remained together on best work only. I looked more like an office worker than a brick layer at the end of the day my shoes were as clean as when I started.

We had a letter from brother George saying he was coming to join us. Lizzie pointed out there would be no room for him with us, so I obtained lodgings for both of us with Mrs. Phillips. She was a widow living two streets away. Her husband had been a Captain in the Merchant Navy and had gone down with his ship. She had a nice house with a bathroom and looked after us very well. She also had a parrakeet which used to screech every morning while we were at breakfast.

There was no more work for George on our firm, but Jack Henshaw offered him a job, chiefly property repairs, until he could find something better. He had travelled down on his motor bike and for a time would join us on our tours around the country-side. The Connors lived opposite, No. 52 Birley Street. They were a very pleasant family, always ready for a 'Do' in the front room, a drink and a game of cards etc. George was introduced to Ada, one of the daughters. I don't know if it was love at first sight, but they spent most of their time together from then on.

It was now late summer and I had an invitation to join the gang on a weekend camping. The father of one of the boys had a large tent. They also had a pony and a costa-mongers cart. We were to load the tent and all our gear on the cart ready to move off after dinner the following Saturday. Our destination was Morton foreshore, where there was a good wide stretch of sand ideal for camping. We were late starting, but we eventually arrived to find we had to negotiate the sand hills to get to our spot. This was slow hard work, and when we suddenly came to a nice level area as it was getting dusk, we decided to set up camp here. It was confusion from then on. We eventually erected the tent with the pony and cart inside. After a supper of sandwiches and a game of cards by candlelight, we attempted to sleep. The pony was very restless and kept stepping on one or the other of the sleepers. Two boxes were holding up the back of the cart. Some of the boys were sleeping on top. The pony knocked the boxes away and the result was a confused heap of boys, shouting and struggling in the dark. Dawn at last. Then suddenly there was a lot of shouting outside and someone was banging on the tent. We crawled to the flap and looked out — a large red faced man, wearing a tweed cap and raincoat, was beating the tent with a walking stick. We were on the Golf Course and our tent was on the 9th Hole. Camping was added to my list of non-activities.

Meanwhile work on the school had proceeded steadily. The main structure finished, tradesmen began to drift away. Ted, my friend and counsellor was moved to another site. I was left on my own for a few weeks 'finishing off'.

The foreman came to me one day and told me William Moss & Sons were building some new tram sheds in Notty Ash, Liverpool. He knew the foreman and if I cared to try for a job with them I could use his name. It was the usual question and answers but O.K. start tomorrow. This was all first class work and thanks to Ted's teaching I fell into it right away. I was given plenty of time to do my work and in return they expected a first class job. I had been there a few weeks when a young chap came to join me. His home was in Wem, Shropshire and he was lodging in Liverpool, but went home for weekends. He told me part of his home town was built on salt mines and the houses were leaning quite a few degrees. I accepted his invitation to see for myself. After work one Saturday I took him home on my pillion seat. His parents made me welcome. We had a pleasant weekend and I was very interested in the leaning houses.

When the main walls were finished two of us were put on to building the boiler house. I was then left on my own to build the chimney stack which was to go up to about 40 feet. After the first two lifts the scaffolders fixed up pulley blocks and a small cradle. My labourer now had no need to climb ladders. He put the bricks and mortar in the cradle and I unloaded at the top. At the end of the day I would send my tool-bag down then the cradle would come up for me.

This arrangement worked well until one Saturday — Liverpool were playing Everton; a local Derby. I promised to go with my mate from Wem. We were to meet at the site entrance at 12 o'clock. A few minutes before time I cleaned up and sent my tool bag down and back came the cradle for me. I noticed two scaffolders stacking some planks. They would take a plank between them, swing it, and on the word 'right' let it go to alight neatly on the stack. When the whistle blew to knock off, I called to my mate. A voice answered 'right' and I stepped into the cradle then — swish — the loose ends of the rope my mate was holding suddenly shot out of his hands. He managed to grab it and stopped me about 10 inches from the ground, but it had taken the skin off the inside of both of his hands. I had had a lucky escape. After first aid to his hands I proceeded to meet my friend at the site entrance. A tram took us to the ground and after a large mug of hot tea and two eccles cakes we settled down to watch the match.

Brother George was not happy on the buildings and eventually managed to get a job with a firm of Civil Engineers, driving an excavator on the new airport at Speke.

For Christmas and New Year 1924–5 I decided to stay in Seacombe and accepted an invitation to the Henshaw's and the Hendersons. We had a very pleasant Christmas and by tradition a large crowd gathered at the Pierhead for the New Year Celebrations. The area was floodlit and we danced the old year out and the new year in.

With my work finished on the tram shed the firm sent me to help on the new store they were building in the town centre for George Henry Lee. This was a large reinforced concrete shell with an outer casing of white buff bricks. The foreman told me to join the other bricklayer on the side wall. He said you can get to him through a window opening on the third floor where I found him easily enough and after the usual introductions he explained what he was doing. Then he said, 'You can take the other end mate, just jump down.' Obeying his instructions I jumped and my heart came into my mouth as the scaffold left the building. I could feel myself hurling to the street, over 50 feet below. Then it came back gently to rest at the side of the building. My head was spinning as my new mate called out, 'Sorry I forgot to tell you we are on a swing scaffold.' It was a platform suspended by two wire ropes and would swing out and back at the slightest movement.

To me this was a very interesting job. It was an opportunity to study this new method of reinforced concrete building, and I was assured it would replace bricks in the near future. However like all the others, this job came to an end. Looking through the papers I was surprised to see a few more adverts for 'Brickies wanted'. One firm was even offering 3d per hour above the rate. Arthur Henderson was looking for a job at the time, so I took him on the pillion to the site. The boss man was a big chap and assured us we could have the extra 3d if we could earn it. So we started next day. The boss was a bricklayer and worked with us. When pay day came however we had only got the standard rate. He said you're not fast enough. I pointed out that we were as fast as him. He said 'That's not the point' so an argument followed. I forgot Townsend's advice and lost my temper. He called me a little so and so but the names I called him suggested he was born out of wedlock. Then using his trowel as a sword, he charged and it was all over in a few seconds. Taking a backward step, he fell over a heap of bricks and complained he had hurt his back so that was the end of the fight and, as he still refused to pay the higher rate, also the end of the job. Arthur's father was a brickie. He was working on a contract in town and Arthur joined him. Jack Henshaw asked me to help with the brickwork on two pairs of houses. It was May 1926 and we suddenly found ourselves in the middle of a National Strike. Everything came to a standstill. All forms of transport stopped and it seemed as though every working man in the country was on strike in sympathy with the miners' claim for a living wage.

The National effort only lasted ten days and in the end the miners had to return to work, but still with no increase in pay.

It only took a few weeks to do the brickwork for Henshaws and I was on the lookout again. I saw a display card in the Labour Exchange. Bricklayers wanted, new housing site, St. Helens. Top rate of pay. Thinking, here we go again, I obtained a green card from the clerk and arranged to go on the Monday. Saturday afternoon with some of the gang at the Swimming Baths we were larking about I jumped in at the shallow end, misjudged the depth and landing badly I strained my ankle. I rested it all day on the Sunday, but Monday it was very painful and I decided I should have to go to St. Helens by train. Arriving at St. Helens I left my tool bag and case at the station and set out to look for the site. Luckily for me it was not too far. After hearing my story the foreman advised me to try to get lodgings nearby and if I felt fit enough I could start next day. There was a row of terrace houses adjoining the site and starting with the first one I thought I would work my way along. I was nearly to the end before I had any luck. An old couple named Grey told me they had a spare bedroom. It's not much but you can go up and have a look. I liked the look of the old people. The living room was spick and span while a nice fire was burning in the grate. I said I would take it. We talked about terms, etc., over a cup of tea and a thick slice of rice cake. Mr. Grey helped me with my case and tool bag from the station. After supper, in answer to their enquiry, I told them about my ankle. She said 'eh lad, Dad'll soon fix that.' She poured some hot water from the kettle standing by the fire into a large saucepan and putting this on the fire said, 'That'll not take long,' Dad came in with an armful of green leaves and as the pan began to boil he put in the leaves, poking them down with a large wooden spoon. I was ordered to bed and as my ankle was very painful I was glad to go. About 20 minutes later they came in with something on a tray. For one dreadful moment I thought it was a Haggis and I had to eat it, but it was put on my ankle and secured with a towel. It was hot, almost more than I could bear. A few minutes later there was a hot cup of cocoa, made with milk, and before long the pain began to ease and I drifted into a sound sleep.

I was suddenly awakened by a loud clatter below my bedroom window. It was daylight and popping over to the window I looked down. The noises had now increased and I saw the street was full of women, wearing long skirts, black shawls, head scarves and clogs. The metal tips of the clogs clicked on the cobbled stones of the street. They were chattering away and calling to each other as they hurried along. In a few minutes they were gone. I heard later they worked for the firm that made Beecham's Pills — worth a guinea a box. Turning to walk back to my bed I suddenly remembered my ankle. The poultice had come off in the night. The pain had completely gone. I stamped my foot on the floor, the ankle was quite sound and my spirits rose as I went down to breakfast. The Greys didn't know the correct name for the plant they used to make the poultice, but they called it 'Knit Bone'. The foreman seemed a little surprised when I turned up for work but when I told him about the 'Knit Bone' he said 'Oh yes, of course, the locals cure most of their ailments with that.' I got on well with the firm. They expected a day's work of course, but it wasn't quite the mad scramble one had got used to on cottage slogging, and as the pay was good I was in no hurry to move on.

St. Helens was quite dull with very little entertainment apart from the cinema. I spent most weekends in Seacombe with my mates.

During October 1926 I saw an advertisement in the Liverpool Echo for a young bricklayer, experienced in jobbing and general building repairs. Good rate of pay, no lost time during bad weather etc. Apply Dabell and Chuck, Crooked Lane, Liverpool.

I had promised to go home for my 21st birthday. I finished at St. Helens, said goodbye to the Greys and was about to start my journey home when I saw the advert. So I made a quick dash to town to see Dabell & Chuck. I had some experience of property repairs with my friend Jack Henshaw. I found Crooked Lane in one of the poorer parts, adjoining dockland. Mr. Dabell was a most unusual type for a builder being dressed in a pin striped suit, smart polished shoes, starched white collar, bowler hat and carrying a furled umbrella. The firm occupied two floors in a large warehouse. These were used as workshop and builders' yard with a small office in one corner. The property in this area was in a poor state of repair, with narrow streets and three and four storey buildings, all holding each other up. An ideal setting for any 'Charles Dickens' story. I was early, but I didn't have to wait long for Mr. Dabell. After the usual conversation it was agreed I should have the job. I explained about my visit home, and he agreed I could start work on my return in a few days time.

The journey home was uneventful. Mother had booked the Village Hall and invited all my old friends, including the Townsends. I knew nothing about this of course. After tea we had dancing and a few drinks and a good time was had by one and all — a very pleasant 21st birthday. After giving a progress report I had a few days holiday and then back to Liverpool to Messrs. Dabell and Chuck. The boss introduced my new mate. He said 'This is 'Sleepy', not much to look at but you will find him a reliable and willing worker.' Sleepy was about 35, 5ft. 10ins. with dark hair and very large hands. His clothes were at least two sizes too big and his eyes about the strangest I had ever seen. They had an upward turn as if he was looking up at the peak of his cap. Mr. Dabell said 'He doesn't talk much, do you Sleepy?' To this,

Sleepy replied 'Ugh'. I didn't like the way things were going, but decided to give it a try. The work was explained in more detail and I was given a list of jobs. We loaded the truck and away we went, with Sleepy as my guide. Sure enough he knew his way around all the back streets, some of which I wouldn't like to travel on my own or after dark. The second week I was called into the office where it was explained that some of the work called for a bit of carpentry, plumbing, glazing, painting, etc. It was too costly to send another tradesman, so would I try and cope. I only had a general idea of the other trades, but I was on my own, it was going to be fun finding out. I liked the variety and soon settled down to being a Jack-of-all-trades. Sleepy was well known in the neighbourhood so we never went short of a cup of tea, packet of cigarettes, etc.

About a week before Christmas we were working at the Fruit Exchange. One room in this building was set out with tables like a market stall. Samples of fruit were set out for the wholesalers to sample. The Auctioneers would then sell the ship's cargo of fruit on the spot. The wholesaler had to collect it and distribute it to the retailer. The caretaker in charge of the stalls gave us permission to take as much as we liked. We stocked up with fruit and nuts for Christmas. I always wore a bib and brace overalls for work. When we had a job at the 'Libro' factory the manager noticed I was always wearing a pair of their own 'Libro' brand. As I was leaving at the end of the job he presented me with a parcel which contained two pairs of overalls. Sleepy lived up to his reputation and his only attempt at conversation was 'Ugh'.

Everything was going well when we were sent to do some roof repairs on some shop property near the Town Centre. It was considered too risky to work off ladders so I decided to use the skylight. Sleepy knew the procedure. I wore an old pair of plimsolls and walked over the roof. Sleepy stood on some steps with his head and shoulders out of the skylight holding a stout rope tied to my waist. I had been working away for about ten minutes when I stepped on to a loose slate. Suddenly my feet shot up into the air and I was sliding down the roof flat on my back. I shouted 'Sleepy'. No answer, not even an 'Ugh'. I came to rest with my feet in the gutter but it was an old cast iron gutter, almost rusted through, and I could feel it crumbling under my feet. Below was a

50 foot drop on to a cobbled yard. The thought of dropping on to that yard made me sweat. 'Sleepy' I called. Still no reply. I lay quite still wondering what to do next. If the rotten gutter gave way I would shoot over the edge and I began to tremble at the thought. If I pulled on the rope and the end came down, no-one would be able to pull me up. My arms were outstretched with my palms flat on the slates. Slowly I drew them in to my sides and with a little pressure I eased my weight off the gutter. Then, slowly, inch at a time, I began to work my way back up towards the skylight, using my back and shoulders. The lump on the back of my head felt as big as an egg. After what seemed like hours, I felt my head touch the skylight cill. Turning quickly I grabbed the cill. I was safe. Lowering myself onto the steps, my legs shaking so much, I thought the steps would topple over. At last I was down. I flopped onto the bare floor and sat down for a moment to recover. I was thinking of something nasty to say to Sleepy when I heard his footsteps on the stairs. His face was distorted into what he intended as a smile. He was carrying two hot cups of tea. I couldn't say anything as I drank my tea and then my eyes followed the rope along the floor to a chisel driven firmly into the brickwork to which the rope was securely tied. I had been safe all the time. I could have pulled myself up had I known the rope was secure, but all Sleepy could say was 'Ugh'. Dabell and Chuck owned some cottage property in the suburb and one day, armed with a list of jobs and our truck well loaded, we set off for the cottages. Mr. Dabell said he would be calling in to see us later. While we were unloading the truck a young woman called to say tea was ready. She was about 35, neatly dressed and with a pleasant smile. Sleepy led the way and sat down at the table without even an 'Ugh'. Then I got the shock of my life for she said 'You know Sleepy's my husband, I suppose?' I thought she was joking, but she went on to tell me he once had a good job on the Dock-Board. That was when they were first married. She told me proudly he was a smart man in those days but that was before the illness struck him. Mr. Dabell is a good friend of ours. He gave Sleepy a job and he's now a regular caller for his cup of tea. With a big smile Sleepy said 'Ugh'.

I enjoyed my work with Dabell and Chuck. I was well paid and with a regular pay packet each week I had managed to save quite a

few pounds. I had been with the firm a little over six months with
Sleepy as my only companion, and I was beginning to feel the
need of younger company, so I didn't hesitate when Arthur
said he could get me a job with him. They were working on a site
at Speke not far from the airfield. His Dad, Bob Jones, Fred and
Uncle Jack, who was temporarily short of work were all in the
same gang. It was quite a long ride to the site and we usually
filled a tram with our gang. I didn't like the work much, but I
was happy to be working with my old mate, and decided this
would do until something better turned up. The tram stop was
just past the entrance to the ferryboat and we would jump off
before it stopped and run down the gangway onto the boat. I
had only been on this job a few weeks when one evening, as we
were running as usual to the boat Arthur stumbled and fell.
Thinking he would get up and catch us, we ran on just before
the gangplank went up. As he wasn't on the boat I concluded
he would have to wait ten minutes for the next. When I saw
Uncle Jack a little later however, he had the worst possible news.
My mate, Arthur Henderson, was dead.

He had died from a heart attack while running for the boat. His
parents told me he had suffered from heart trouble since he was
about six years old. The Doctor had told them that with care, he
could live for years, but as there was no cure, they must always be
prepared. I, of course, knew nothing of all this and felt numb with
the shock. The next few weeks were very sad. Bill Henderson came
back to work after the funeral, but he was a changed man and
looked ten years older. The foreman on this job was a crafty old
devil. He would get two pairs of houses up to 'wall plate', that is
only the four chimney stacks to build and then, when the scaffold
to each was loaded he would call to four young brickies, 'OK, get
them up.' The four selected would grab their toolbags and run up
the ladder frantically to see who could finish first. The last could
expect his cards at the end of the week. That was just one of the
tricks. They would set on anyone who applied for work and then,
at the end of the week, there would be a wholesale sacking.

Jack Henshaw started courting and I began to see less and less
of him. This was a very unhappy period for me. In this great City,
with nearly seven million [sic] busy people I felt very much alone. I
was happier as a boy roaming the fields with only the birds and

bees for company. Now laughter was hard to come by. During the following weeks I became more restless and finally decided it was time to move. Always at the back of my mind was a picture of the Cransley Reservoir and the windmill across the meadows in the countryside I loved. Once having made my mind up, I lost no time. I said my goodbyes to all my friends and relations. With my case packed I once more made for the open road, but this time I was going home.

CHAPTER IV
Home Again

Mother soon filled me in with all the local news. I learned that Loddington was to have four new council houses. A builder from Kettering had the contract and work was about to start. I decided however, before looking for a job I would have a few days holiday. It was early summer and the countryside was at its best. I walked along by the side of the brook that fed the Cransley Reservoir, past the old windmill, until I came to the footbridge to Marriotts Mill. I sat down in the long grass and to the gentle ripple of the stream allowed my thoughts to wander back over the years when we were kids at school and the games we used to play. I don't remember buying any marbles for we had a plentiful supply of blue clay in the ironstone mines and we made our own with two pieces of flat board. We rolled the clay to the various sizes and then, at convenient times, we popped them into the oven. The next painting lesson at school was devoted to colouring our marbles. "Katty" was another summer game. You need a piece of wood about 4 inches long and 1 inch round, pointed at each end and also a cane or thick peg about 2 foot long. You tap the pointed end when the Katty would jump up and you then strike it while its in mid-air. Dangerous if there are many windows about. Five stones was a favourite game for boys. You throw five small stones in the air and the points were counted by the number you caught on the back of your hand, and then, of course, conkers in the Autumn. The girls were content with hop scotch and the skipping rope.

I knew Mill Farm well enough. It was situated in a very remote spot between Loddington and Cransley. Often after school, Mother would say, 'pop over to the Mill for a can of milk. Get as much as you can for 2d.' Old Miss Marriott, the farmer's sister would say, 'I'm glad you've come boy. Just do a little job for me, it won't take long.' It would often be an hour later before I could start back but I didn't mind as I would have a full can of milk and still have the 2d. On one occasion the farmer sent me to Broughton to get one of the horses shod. On arrival at the blacksmiths I found them busy making a set of heavy harrows. 'Just hang on boy we shan't be long.' It was an hour before they started on my horse and quite dark when they finished. Mother was waiting at the old footbridge and getting quite worried, but I was happy, I had a full can of milk and still had the 2d.

But what of today? As I sat there I became aware of a new sound. The tractor had taken the place of horses and I could hear two of them at work in adjoining fields. The farmers were going to market in their motor cars – the pony and trap had gone. Mr. Davenport still had ponies to do the bread round, but he had a Model T Ford to do the Kettering journeys. I was told, when he was learning to drive, he would pull on the steering wheel and shout 'Whoa' when he wanted to stop.

As I wandered around the village the people I met seemed older. I didn't know any of the children and many things had changed in six years.

The building trade was busy and there had been a general increase in wages. Everyone had a wireless set and quite a few more made weekly visits to the cinema. The cinema at Rothwell was well patronised with prices ranging from 4d to 10d. We were used to seeing the silent films with piano or organ accompaniment. Al Jolson and Sonny Boy put a stop to all that and talkies were taking over.

I met my old friend John Church and he told me about a new sport at the White City, London which was Greyhound Racing. John was now married and had started a family. He was also a businessman, having acquired a hairdressing salon in London. He insisted I should spend a weekend with them as soon as possible.

I met Mr. T. G. Barlow, the builder, who had the Loddington contract. He had several jobs in Kettering to finish before he could start on our council houses. We discussed rates and I agreed to start right away. He was a tall man about 35 years old, a carpenter by trade. After a few weeks in Kettering we were to start at Loddington. There was no water on the site, so before we could start building we had to sink a well. This was a new experience for me. Luckily I didn't suffer from claustrophobia because

Arthur in 1929.

twenty feet looking up seems a lot further than twenty feet looking down. At this depth we struck ironstone and this called for heavy hammers and chisels. I was working away when a large chisel came hurling down. It flicked the peak of my cap and struck the rock at my feet; just one inch nearer it would have gone through my head. My labourer had left the chisel near the edge of the well and when the children came out of school, it needed only a touch to send it down. Another narrow escape! Eventually we found water and after I had bricked up the well we were able to proceed with the houses.

Greyhound Racing was started on the Kettering football ground. My boss was an enthusiast so we had something else in common. John Church was soon on the scene. He brought his dogs from London and had quite a few wins. It was not long before I was the proud possessor of two dogs. 'Pongo' was a large brindle dog and 'White Collar' a light brown bitch with a white band around her neck. Keith Bellamy, the son of the landlady at the New Inn, had a car and with our dogs we visited all the local tracks. Sometimes as far afield as Leicester, Coalville and Northampton. It was all exciting and good fun but, like the horse racing, I didn't have much luck; in fact the only time my dog won at Kettering I was in bed with a severe cold and I was not there to back it. Greyhound racing was all the rage at that time and as I had no difficulty in finding buyers for my two dogs; the sport was then crossed off my list.

Cricket was more in my line. I joined the club and spent most of my spare time getting back into practice. I had another sideline when Mother and I went into partnership keeping pigs. I looked after them, feeding morning and evening, while she prepared the food — boiling potatoes, kitchen scraps, etc., to mix with the meal. Life was passing pleasant.

I had been with Mr. Barlow about eighteen months when I saw an advert in the paper for bricklayers to work on the railway. In due course I had an interview with a Mr. Stretton. He explained that the Company had in the past employed contractors to do all the maintenance on railway property. They had decided now to employ their own tradesmen and it was his job to engage a team for this purpose. I had a letter about two weeks later saying my application had been accepted. I was to report to Mr. Stretton giving full details where and when etc. I arrived at his office to find about a dozen men standing around talking. I was called in and learned that Mr. Stretton was a Permanent Way Inspector and knew nothing about building repairs. As I had had some experience I had been selected to help him to get the scheme underway. He told me I was to have the rank of Sub-Inspector, (unpaid) and after a period of satisfactory employment the appointment would be confirmed, with a suitable increase in wages. I was satisfied with this and we soon got organised. After about six months I was summoned to the Head Office in Northampton. After waiting for an hour I was taken into the 'Big Man' himself. He was a retired Army Colonel, white hair and moustache etc. After a long rigmarole, he confirmed my status and asked if there was anything I wished to say. It was then I think, I spoiled what might have developed into a beautiful friendship. I said 'How much?' His manner changed immediately and, after a long pause, it transpired I was to receive an increase of 1/6d per week. I thanked him in a manner I thought fitting to the occasion, and asked for time to consider. At the back of my mind, I had ideas I thought would bring in more than 1/6d per week.

Back at Kettering however, I gave Mr. Stretton an account of the interview. I told him I was not interested in the Sub-Inspector's job and would he please look for someone else. About that time the Kettering bricklayers and labourers joined the Northampton Gang on extensive repairs to Corby Tunnel. This involved a 12 hour Sunday shift and, at double time, this was a substantial increase in the pay packet.

Our territory included all stations from Kettering to North-ampton, Wellingborough, Leicester, Oakham, Stamford and Cambridge. Much of the work was at small wayside stations and, owing to the infrequency of the trains, we were ordered to lodge out. For this we received lodging allowance, basket money and tool money etc. Petrol was about 10½d per gallon so I used my motorbike and managed to get home every evening. This happy state of affairs continued for about four years. During that time my social life was good. Although I was not up to the required standard for football, I took a close interest in the team. Cricket was my game and I seldom missed a match. Dancing was also high on my list and in the October Desborough Feast, there was always a grand dance. For this occasion our gang attended. Towards the close I noticed a girl I thought very easy on the eye. She was very pretty, with big blue eyes. The band was playing, 'Let me call you Sweetheart'. I didn't get a chance to speak to her that evening but on the following Sunday evening, I was having a drink with one of my mates in the Palm Lounge, at the Royal Hotel, when she came in with a party of friends. This time I not only got a word in but I managed to fix up a meeting for later in the week. 'In the Spring a young man's fancy lightly turns to thoughts of love.' I was proud to take my new girl home to meet the family. She became a regular spectator at the cricket matches and took part in organising the dances and enjoyed village life to the full. We had a lot in common; cycling and a love of the countryside. I taught her how to plait corn and make corn dollies which was something I had learned when I was a fully paid up cow minder. It was after one of our country rides when we called in at the jewellers and I invited her to choose a ring that we became engaged. This was a happy period for us. We started at once to make plans for the wedding and laughter was easy to come by.

We married on Christmas Eve, 24th December 1932, at Kettering Parish Church. Father Kingdom officiated and the sun shone like summer. Both families were well represented at the wedding and we danced to the end of the perfect day. Christmas morning was again fine and sunny so we walked to Loddington and arrived in time to join the family for Christmas dinner. So started our married life. We had already decided not to have a honeymoon and would put the money towards a new house. We had rented two rooms and furnished them to our taste. We were both happy to go back to work and start saving for the future but then we had the first shock! The Railway Company had started a new economy drive. No more Sunday work at double time and no lodging out so we had to travel back by train every day. The working hours were cut and my wages were down to £2.9s. per week. There was plenty of building going on at the time so I said goodbye to the Railway Company and started on the new bus station in Northampton Road. This brought my wages to a little over £3.10s. per week.

About a year later, I was working for a building firm from

Arthur's fiancée — Miss Violet Goode of Kettering.

Burton Latimer building houses and flats. The plans showed a row of lock-up garages, and I offered to do the brickwork – sub-contract, in my own time. My offer was accepted and for the next few weeks my evenings and weekends were devoted to these. Meantime the Doctor had confirmed that, in the not too distant future, we could expect to hear the patter of tiny feet. Our first baby was on the way. Our happiness however was marred by the fact that Mother, who had been poorly for some time, was not responding to treatment, and we were all very concerned. After a serious operation in Northampton General Hospital we began to feel that there was hope of her recovery. My sister Alice was a wonderful nurse but all her care and devotion was to no avail. Mother's condition deteriorated and she died a few weeks before our son was born. On her death my thoughts went back over the years, and to the little chapel where we used to sing –

> When I was but a little child,
> How well I recollect,
> How oft I vexed my Mother,
> With my folly and neglect, etc.

Our Mother was the foundation stone to our family. When she died it was a loss to us all, from which we never really recovered.

I was soon to become a family man, and the need for suitable accomodation was getting urgent. My search led me to a double fronted stone house in the Town Centre, with a large garden and workshop. If I was to carry out my plan, to start in business on my own, this was the ideal situation. As soon as terms were agreed and with the help of the Building Society I became the new owner.

Our baby came on the 28th March 1934 – a boy. I worked hard on modernising and decorating the house and in a few weeks we were able to move in. I was, of course, still working as a bricklayer for the Burton Latimer firm but all my spare time was spent converting the garden into a builders yard and workshop. One evening a young chap came to see me. He explained he was an electrician about to start on his own. He specialized in neon signs and would fix a sign for me at cost price. I agreed to this and a week later 'A. E. STURGESS, BUILDING CONTRACTOR', appeared in flashing neon lights – the first in town.

If I had expected customers to queue up for my services I

should have been disappointed. I did have a bit of luck however which was to give me a start.

I was having a Sunday lunchtime drink in the Argyll Club, with my father-in-law, when a well dressed man came over to our table. He was an Estate Agent and he explained that he had a client on his book who needed a builder to build a bungalow on his own land, was I interested? I was. When all the details were settled. I ordered the materials, handed in my notice and I was away. I had started on my own. I didn't make much profit on my first contract, but I didn't mind. I had a lot to learn and I was learning fast.

The Agent invited me to have a drink with him in the Royal Hotel. He said you will meet the right kind of people here and they will be quite helpful when you get to know them. There was a room behind the Bar — 'Men Only', also the billiard room, where the business men of the town used to meet. I was introduced to Bank Managers, Lawyers, Architects, Accountants, Department Bosses from Stewarts & Lloyds etc. I had my half of beer and listened to their conversations. I was finding out how the other half lived. During the following weeks I became a regular caller at the Royal for a game of billiards and to get better acquainted.

One evening a Stewarts & Lloyds' man asked me if I knew where he could get a good sectional hut for his garden. He explained that Stewarts & Lloyds were importing a lot of families from the North. They were satisfied with the houses but there were no outside buildings — not even a garden shed. I promised to look into this and let him know. I had received a small contract to build six lock-up garages at the north end of town. A carpenter at Rothwell had just started on his own, and he agreed to supply and fix the folding doors. I outlined the idea of the garden sheds in which he was very interested and, after a full discussion, he submitted a list of sizes and prices, ex works. I was to deliver and erect. I had some coloured leaflets printed illustrating our garden shed and these were distributed on the new estates at Corby. Also a nice big advert in the local paper, and sure enough, the orders began to arrive at a good rate. In the meantime, I finished the brickwork on the garages and was waiting for the carpenter to fix the doors. After several reminders he promised to get extra help and start on the job the following Saturday, and he would finish the doors over the weekend. With this promise I went ahead and fixed the corrugated asbestos roof. The result was the carpenter failed to turn up and on the Sunday evening we had a terrific storm. The strong wind got in where the doors should have been and lifted the whole roof off, smashing the asbestos sheets in the process. I fixed another roof after the doors were put on, but I think I said something that offended the carpenter. He refused to carry on with the shed contract and I was left with over thirty orders to fulfill. There was only one way I could see and that was to do them myself, so I ordered a load of timber and set about my task, but the orders came in too fast for me to cope. I engaged a carpenter and an apprentice. I then bought a secondhand drop sided Ford lorry and with a boy to assist, I delivered and erected as fast as the carpenter could make them up.

One evening in the Royal I was advised to call on the Estate Administrator for Stewarts and Lloyds at Corby. He explained that the company owned about 20 army huts on a site close to the main offices. They were occupied by Stewarts and Lloyds employees and needed extensive repairs. I engaged a lorry driver to take over the hut deliveries and found myself needing some form of transport. I settled on a 12 h.p. bullnosed Morris coupé. The asking price was £13.10s. and eventually I became the proud owner at £12.10s. cash.

We had a wedding in the family that day. My wife's brother was getting married at Rothwell. Taking the baby she went on ahead and I followed in the car. When it was time to leave we found ourselves in a thick fog, a real pea-souper. The headlights were useless and I began to think we wouldn't make it when, in thick mist, I spotted the lights of a United Counties bus. I tucked in behind this and we crawled back to Kettering in low gear. At the bottom of Hospital Hill, the car coughed and then stopped because we were out of petrol. We carried the baby home and I went back later with a can of petrol. We called our car 'Widow Twanky'. We didn't get off to a very good start, but in the months that followed she proved to be a good investment. All she needed was petrol and water with an occasional pint of oil. The family two doors away had a teenage daughter who came in as babysitter so this enabled us to get out for one evening a week. Our favourite outing was to ride to one of the village pubs where we could join

Arthur with his first car (Widow Twankey) in 1934.

in the sing-song around the piano. My wife had a very pleasant voice and was in great demand on these occasions. We would then drive slowly home down the country lanes singing such old favourites as 'Moonlight and Roses' etc.

'Life was passing pleasant'.

I bought a single plot of land in Boddington Road and Mr. Surridge (of Gotch, Sanders & Surridge, Architects) whom I had met in the Royal prepared plans for a bungalow. Whilst this was going on I bought a larger plot, big enough to hold six houses, from a market gardener who was retiring, for £35. We obtained Council approval and were able to go straight on with these. The Co-op bought the first two before they were completed and converted them into shops.

The Women's Suffragette Movement, started in the 1920's, was getting stronger; in 1929 Margaret Bondfield became the first woman Cabinet Minister. The Government were pressed into starting the Slum Clearance Programme and the building trade was getting busy. By 1936 we had built 12 houses and a bungalow in Boddington Road.

In the meantime I had received a letter from Stewarts & Lloyds. They had provided housing accommodation for the tenants of the army huts and I was to give a price for clearing the whole site. Making allowance for the materials, this was a very lucrative venture for me. I supplied and erected one of the huts for a furnishing Company to use as a warehouse. With the materials off the site we erected a tennis and cricket pavilion for Stewarts and Lloyds on the sports ground in Occupation Road. I advertised the remainder for sale in the local paper and the purchaser was to dismantle and remove. The result was very satisfactory and in a few weeks the site was cleared.

My wife had taken a fancy to one of the houses in Boddington Road so I let our house to the lorry driver and moved in. About this time I bought a new Bedford lorry; had it painted red, white and blue and entered it in the Carnival celebrating the coronation of King George VI. (Edward VIII having abdicated with Mrs. Simpson.)

We were now quite busy with houses built to order in Kettering and Geddington, property repairs etc. I still called in at the Royal whenever I had time to catch up with the latest information and it was in here that I heard of a piece of land for sale on the Rockingham Road, Corby. Eventually I managed to buy this and Gotch, Sanders and Surridge prepared plans for 60 houses and 8 shops and flats. I advertised in the usual way with coloured leaflets and in the local papers. Enquiries soon began to pour in, and we had thirty seven contracts signed before we laid a brick.

My next letter from Stewarts & Lloyds was to invite me to tender for the building of the football stand on the Occupation Road sports field. Our price was accepted a few weeks later and we started work as soon as the materials arrived. We were now very busy, too busy in fact to take any notice when Hitler occupied the Rhineland.

A well-dressed young man engaged me in conversation one evening in the Royal. He was Assistant Manager in one of the larger furnishing companies. He wanted to start on his own account but was short of capital. He had the idea of furnishing a show house on our estate. This was something new at that time and I was very interested. We met again a few days later and went further into the details with the result that I rented a shop in the Jamb, Corby. My new friend furnished it and changed the sign to 'The Corby Furnishing Co'. As soon as the first house was ready we used it as a show house. It was then furnished by our new Company. During the months that followed we had a steady stream of prospective purchasers through the show house. I had engaged an experienced clerk for my office as the paper work was now too much for me in the evenings and, with a foreman to look after the site work, all the jobs were running smoothly.

Widow Twanky had been a good and faithful servant, but the time had come to make a change. My choice was a 12 h.p. OHV Singer. I was not able to leave my business for long, but when the new car was run-in, we took a long weekend off to visit our relations in Liverpool. Ten years had passed and many changes had been made. There was much more motor traffic and the new Mersey tunnel was coping with this. We drove through the tunnel just to see what it was like. During our stay we also crossed the river on the ferryboat and paid a visit to the Cathedral. My wife was very impressed, but John took it all in his stride. We managed a quick run up to Llandudno, but then it was back home to work. The car had behaved very well and we had all enjoyed our short holiday.

The football stand was completed in time to start the new football Season and I was invited to attend the grand opening arranged by Stewarts & Lloyds.

All the shops and flats on the Rockingham Road were sold; some were occupied and we were working hard to complete the remainder. In the meantime we had started on three larger houses built to order on the Northampton Road, Kettering. Gotch, Sanders and Surridge were the Architects for Corby Council and we were invited to tendor for 40 houses on the Oakley Road Site together with all roads and sewers etc.

The show house on the estate had been a great success and only a few plots now remained unsold. Our social life was good and we managed to get a week at the seaside. Dancing was high on the list and we also had a long weekend with John Church and family. He took us to the White City Greyhound racing where my wife was on top of the world having backed four winners. After a visit to the doctor my wife was able to confirm that John would soon have a little playmate. This news made us very happy but this time of course we wanted a girl.

In the Royal the talk was about the possibility of War with the muddle of Czechoslovakia and later the confusion of Poland after Hitler had stated he had no territorial claims in Europe. News filtered through the grape-vine that Stewarts and Lloyds had stopped their house building programme and were making preparations for war. I had a letter from the architects saying that Corby Council had taken 40 surplus houses from Stewarts and Lloyds and would not now proceed with the Oakley Road Scheme. This was a big disappointment and as there was no new work starting up we had to reduce our labour force.

Like many others the war came at a very bad time for me. My business that I had worked so hard to establish had to be disbanded and our whole way of life was to be changed as we prepared for War. I was 34 years old and expected to be in an early call-up. Our daughter was born 26th August 1939, (Happy). Chamberlain the Prime Minister announced 'we are at war with Germany' on 3rd September, 1939.

Arthur and Violet Sturgess with their children, John and Mary, in 1940.

POSTSCRIPT

During his years immediately prior to World War II, trading under his own name, Arthur Sturgess built large detached houses to individual architects' designs, several of which stand on the outskirts of Kettering on each side of the A43 Kettering–Northampton Road. At the outbreak of war many young men from the building trades were conscripted into the Forces and the company was engaged on Government contracts, building airfields, air-raid shelters etc.

When the war ended he was involved with the expansion of Corby where many houses were under construction, but after a post-war holiday at Skegness he bought an hotel called the Welbeck, refurbished it and after about a year sold that and bought a larger hotel called Trees.

Returning to Northamptonshire in the early 1950s, the pleurisy which he had suffered from as a young man in Liverpool returned, and on doctor's advice he regretfully left the building trade.

As a completely new venture he opened a shoe closing unit in Rothwell, assembling shoe uppers for several factories of well known footwear manufacturers in the County.

This business prospered, employing at its peak about twenty-five machinists, keeping him busily engaged until his retirement in 1977.

He died in July, 1979, aged seventy-three.